CHRONICLES OF OLD SAN FRANCISCO
EXPLORING THE HISTORIC CITY BY THE BAY

GAEL CHANDLER

© 2014 Gael Chandler
© 2014 Museyon

Published in the United States by:
Museyon, Inc.
2 W. 46th St., Mezz. 209
New York, NY 10036

Museyon is a registered trademark.
Visit us online at www.museyon.com

ISBN 978-0-9846334-9-4

1456290

Printed in China

To Bob Chandler for first taking me to San Francisco in 1965

and to Denny Chandler for telling me in 1970, "You're dropping out of college and moving to San Francisco where you think the streets are paved with gold and you're going to become a hippie like Margie M," and for hanging in to see where it all led,

and to Sherry Green who walked this book word by word and step by step and with whom living in the Bay Area is always an adventure.

Gael Chandler

CHRONICLES OF OLD SAN FRANCISCO

CHRONICLES OF OLD SAN FRANCISCO

Sites that appear in the chapters

San Francisco

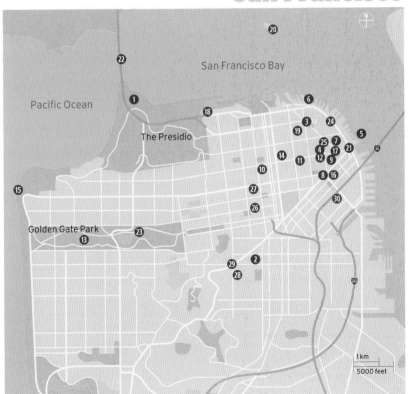

CHAPTER 1.

LIVING ON THE LAND IN PEACE AND FREEDOM: THE YELAMU AND THE EXPEDITION OF JUAN BAUTISTA DE ANZA

1775

The men let their hair grow long. The women didn't always cover their breasts. They went barefoot or wore handmade fiber sandals and lived in cone-shaped houses framed with willow branches and layered with tule reeds on communal land. They made love uninhibitedly, coupling and uncoupling freely. They baked their own bread and picked wild cherries and blackberries from their land. They possessed no weapons. Regularly, they dressed up in feathers and beads to sing and dance all night and day.

No they weren't hippies, they were Yelamu, the 160 original inhabitants of the peninsular thumb of land we call San Francisco. A tribelet of the Ohlone Indians, who numbered up to 10,000, the Yelamu lived for approximately 4,000 years in relative harmony with their neighboring tribelet, intermarrying and settling disputes with exchanges of gifts between chiefs.

They used double paddles to propel their boats of watertight tule reeds through ocean, lake and stream. For the peninsula and 50 hills that make up the 46.9 square miles that is today's city were then comprised of giant sand dunes—many more than 100 feet high. These dunes, along with tidal

Ohlone Indians on tule rafts on San Francisco Bay

marshes, mudflats, and creeks, were also home to wolves, grizzly bear, tule elk, antelope, panthers, and many species of birds. The Yelamu lived in villages located at areas now known as the Presidio, Ocean Beach, Fort Mason, and possibly Alcatraz Island.

Salmon, oyster, deer, rabbit, nuts, seeds, insects, and other local foodstuff nourished them, along with homebrewed beer and Manzanita cider. The Yelamu were steady stewards of the land who routinely pruned and burned shrub, grass, and poison oak to maintain the ecosystem and their food, herb, and medicine supply. They maintained small, seasonal villages as well as a larger, primary village. The work was divided up between shaman, doctors, song leaders, crafters, midwives, and storytellers. The chief hosted visitors and served as speaker and philosopher—overseeing ceremonial functions yet holding little governing power. The leader of each family unit dealt with disputes and rights.

Matrilineal, the Yelamu used shells for currency to cement marriages as well as divorces and to trade with other tribes. They kept their language intact, not learning the language of other Ohlone tribes, with whom they co-existed (with occasional warfare) for centuries. Their middens (garbage mounds) reveal a consistency of diet, basketry, clothing, trade and religious objects over the millennia. When someone died, the Yelamu buried their body or burned it along with their hut and belongings, obliterating all traces of the person and never referring to them again.

It was an extended time of community, peace, tradition, and freedom—the likes of which the city hasn't seen since. But change was on the horizon, literally, with masts of ships, unlike anything the Yelamu had ever seen, approaching the shore.

Beginning in the 1500s, European ships had been plying the Pacific Ocean, some to explore, some to claim land and take spices, gold, and other riches from it, and some to rob these booty-laden ships. The Spanish had claimed the most land and made off with most wealth and this irked the British. Unwilling to make war head on, Queen Elizabeth I endowed sea captains—French and Dutch as well as British— with a Letter of Marque. This effectively licensed these privateers, or buccaneers as they were known, to attack and loot Spanish ships.

In 1579, one such British buccaneer, Sir Francis Drake, was deadheading to England, his ship, the *Golden Hind*, stuffed with plunder. A storm blew his galleon off course and as a respite, he set anchor at an inlet—now called Drake's Bay—near Point Reyes (just north of San Francisco). In the first recorded encounter of cultures, the *Golden Hind*'s chaplain, Francis Fletcher, described the Indians' actions, dress, houses, often with misinterpretation and Christian cultural bias: "They are a people of a tractable, free, and loving nature, without guile or treachery; their bows and arrows (their only weapons and almost all their wealth) they use very skillfully but yet not to do any harm with them being by reason of their weakness, more fit for children than for men."

By 1775, Spain, having won and lost a few battles with England both on land and sea, set its sights on the west coast of the New World, specifically Alta (upper) California. Spain had already planted a string of presidios (forts), pueblos (villages), and missions as far north as Monterey. In addition to the buccaneer raids in the Pacific, the Spanish had other worries: The Russians were running a thriving fur business in Alaska and extending their trading posts south, and France and England were financing explorers to the region to pinpoint the Northwest Passage.

The Spanish crown decided it was time to act. The maps had been drawn and the route defined by

Drake's Landing in California, engraving published 1590 by Theodor de Bry

From left: Juan Bautista de Anza; the route of Anza's expedition

earlier Spanish expeditions. And so Viceroy Antonio Maria de Bucareli's order came down to Juan Bautista de Anza: Claim a site for Spain and Catholicism on San Francisco Bay.

Recently promoted to lieutenant colonel as both reward for past forays—including a reconnaissance trip to San Francisco Bay in 1774—and encouragement for this assignment, Anza did not hesitate to accept.

Born in Fronteras, Sonora, Anza now resided in Tubac, Arizona (all Spanish territory) where his military career had taken him. He prepared methodically, planning his route, gathering five years' worth of supplies, and putting together a party of Franciscan priests, colonists, and soldiers at the presidio in Horcasitas, Sonora. The Spanish crown bolstered his recruitment, providing many enticements: generous amounts of clothing, from sturdy boots to petticoats, as well as chocolate, Castilian wine, 335 cattle, and 695 horses and mules. The historical roster reflects the success of their efforts, totaling 240 people: three Indian interpreters, three padres and their servants, 21 soldiers and their 29 wives, 40 families with 115 children, and 23 wranglers.

On September 29, 1775, Anza shouted the first of many *"¡Vayan subiendos!"* (Mount up everybody!) and the party took off. First stop: Tubac. They holed up in the presidio due to Apache raids on the town, then moved out again on October 23. Within a few days, the group experienced their first death (a mother in childbirth) and new life: her baby survived. Illness—of humans and animals—caused further downtime.

Underway again, Anza led them north through the Maricopa Mountains, then west across the Arizona desert, where, parched and exhausted, they anticipated reaching Yuma and the Colorado River. They made it to the river, only to discover the ford was washed out. Yuma Indians came to their aid, helping scout out a new ford. At last, the expedition crossed the river and arrived in Alta California only to face more desert. They trudged onward to San Sebastian (present day Harper's Well), a sub-sea-level town in the Yuha Desert, where snow and unseasonably frigid weather accosted them. But on they went, making their weary way up Alta California, often short on water. At one dried-up campground most of the thirsty cattle bolted.

Finally, after two and a half months, they reached their first Catholic outpost since Tubac: Mission San Gabriel. The future colonists took a long, much-needed rest, but not the intrepid Anza. He rode his horse south to the San Diego mission to help quell the Indians who had killed its priest and two Spanish workers. He also rounded up more supplies—along with a few soldiers who had stolen provisions and deserted the expedition.

Mission San Gabriel, by Ferdinand Deppe, c. 1832

*Dance of Native Californians at Mission Dolores in 1816,
painted by the Russian artist Ludwig Choris*

Rejuvenated and rejoined with Anza, the group worked its way north, enjoying welcoming stays at Mission San Luis Obispo and Mission San Antonio, and, after 1,500 miles, Mission Monterey. There they rested, waiting for their eventual summons from Anza, who headed north to San Francisco Bay accompanied by one padre (Pedro Font), eight soldiers, and a few regional guides.

On March 28, 1776, on a bluff above the future city, Anza fulfilled his mission: He claimed the land for Spain and designated a site of 90 *varas* (paces) on each side for a presidio. Father Font rhapsodized about his choice: "The commander decided to erect the holy cross on the extremity of the white cliff at the inner point of the entrance to the port—This mesa commands a most wonderful view, since from it a great part of the port is visible, with its islands, the entrance, and the ocean, as far as the eye can reach—it is so commanding that the entrance of the mouth of the port can be defended by musket-fire, and at the distance of a musket-shot there is water for the use of the people..."

Construction began after the arrival of the settlers (grown to 244 now) on June 27. Soldiers forced the Yelamu into laboring for the mission. On September 17, Father Francisco Palóu blessed the newly erected presidio and conducted a mass at a small, wooden church nearby.

By then Anza had de-camped back to Arizona and been boosted to governor by the viceroy. On August 2, 1791, Father Palóu dedicated the completed mission, naming it San Francisco de Asís. Composed of wood, 36,000 adobe bricks, and adobe roof tiles molded on the thighs of Indian women, the Mission Dolores, as it has always been called, still stands today. Despite quakes and renovations, it remains the oldest building in San Francisco. Its cemetery shelters the bones of its creators: settlers, soldiers, Yelamu Indians, and clergy.

PRESIDIO AND CRISSY FIELD

Presidio, c. 1792

Today the Presidio remains a vital part of San Francsico, though the original Spanish fort for which it was named is completely gone. From 1848 throughout much of the 20th century, the Presidio's 1,491 acres served as an important military base, playing a key role during the wars of the Pacific. When it closed in 1995 it was the longest-operating military base in the nation.

Today the military barracks and marching grounds have been transformed into a national park, with a visitors center, museums, hiking and biking trails, beautiful vistas, native plantss and beaches. In addition to its natural splendor, the Presidio is also home to restaurants, residences, and the $300-million headquarters of George Lucas' film company.

Thanks, in part, to support from the National Park Service, the Presidio has undergone a decade-long remediation plan to clean up and preserve the area's natural landscape, uncover creeks and restore marshes—including two tidal marsh ponds on Crissy Field (See Walking Tour #8).

CHAPTER 2.

IN THE TIME OF WINE, ROSES, GRIZZLY BEARS, AND RANCHOS: PIONEER JUANA BRIONES AND MEXICAN CALIFORNIA

1821–1848

Things weren't going so well at the Presidio when Juana Briones was born in 1802. Since her grandparents and her mother made the trek with Anza in 1776, its buildings were deteriorating and the number of potential converts and laborers—the Yelamu Indians of the Ohlone tribe—was dwindling. The shortage of servants had gotten so bad that the Presidio's soldiers were galloping far afield to capture other Ohlone Indians who were retreating to outer areas. It's not that the padres hadn't tried; God knows they'd baptized scores of Yelamu. But the Lord's savage, dim-witted children—as the *misioneros* regarded them—somehow didn't take to imprisonment. Many ran away or otherwise revolted. The soldiers, (who reviled this hardship post, which paid little or nothing), constantly hunted them down, dragged them back to the Presidio, and strapped them into bastinados (fetters). The unmarried women worked all day and were kept sequestered in the name of virginity, making them soldiers' prey also. Annually, a third of the Yelamu population was dying from dysentery, measles, malaria, tuberculosis, syphilis, and other diseases previously unknown to them, as well as from lack of proper medical treatment, beatings, shootings, and despair.

From left: Juana Briones; Presidio and Golden Gate in the Hispanic colonial era, 1817

The Spanish needed to find other ways to maintain a hold on their territory, so in 1784 they instituted the *rancho* (land grant) system. A rancho was a concession of land (located outside the presidio and mission) from the Spanish government (which retained title) that allowed the owner to launch a livelihood—usually cattle grazing—and set down a home. Under the Spanish rules, Briones wouldn't have been eligible for a grant but eventually she would get one and fight a lengthy legal battle to keep it.

In 1820, at the age of 18, Briones married a cavalry soldier and proceeded to have eleven children, seven of whom lived. She raised them along with an orphaned Indian girl she adopted. When her husband's drunken abuse became too much, Briones obtained a clerical divorce and moved her family to a new house on a farm near the Presidio where she grew vegetables and raised cattle.

Although she had no formal education and could neither read nor write, Briones was both a *curandera* (herbalist healer), having learned the practice growing up from Indian and Mexican neighbors, and a bonesetter. Throughout her life she tended all races and occupations of people she encountered, including sailors in port and village Indians. She was also a consummate entrepreneur, aided by the Mexican government's actions during the 1820s and 1830s.

On September 16, 1821, Mexico achieved independence from Spain. With a sweep of the pen, Alta California became a territory of Mexico. By 1828, Mexico had set new rancho rules, designed in part to help Californios—as the settlers now called themselves—obtain land more easily. The Spanish had issued 30 land grants in Alta California; the Mexicans upped this to total to over 800 grants of an average 22,000 acres each. The Mexican government forged these new laws to break the hold the missions had on the land, an effort augmented by The Secularization Act of 1833. The act officially ended the already moribund mission system and ceded the majority of mission land— save for the mission church and priests' residences and gardens—to Mexico.

The act aimed to give small plots to the Indians who deserted the missions in droves. However, most of the land was sold to powerful male Californios of Spanish blood—which Briones had, along with African and Indian blood. She purchased a rancho in San Francisco in a section that would be called North Beach. On her land, documented as Playa de Juana Briones (Juana Briones Beach), she grew vegetables and created a dairy farm. When sailors and merchants came into port, she traded produce and milk with them. She also doctored their ailments and in 1834 crossed the bay to Marin County to help squelch an outbreak of smallpox.

Castilian roses and wines, rodeos (to herd and brand cows), barbeques, and fiestas: It was the heyday of rancho life, with dons running large estates and their wives running the households, both relying on the labor of Indians and mixed blood servants. Rancheros lived in adobe haciendas with tile roofs made of red clay and straw tile, and they planted a cornucopia of trees, plants, flowers, and vines: olive, citrus, peach, pear, fig, grape, hemp, flax, and more. They depended on a large and extended family—twelve to fifteen children comprised a typical brood—for entertainment, though friends and visitors made for more fun and sport on fiesta days.

Herds of grizzly bears marauded the countryside, so pairs of vaqueros (cowboys) hunted them. Each vaquero employed a taut *reata* (a 50- to 60- foot rope made from rawhide or braided horsehair) to lasso the wild beast and parade it around before killing it. On occasion, they tethered the bear's hind foot to a bull's forefoot, staging a fight to the death for a raucous, appreciative crowd.

Regularly, Indian butchers corralled cows and sheep and slaughtered them in a calaveras (place of skulls). Hide and tallow were profitable trade items with the Americans, who were arriving in port and beginning to trickle in

Native Californians lassoing a bear, c. 1873

from overland routes. Briones did her share of commerce with them and doctored their ailments as well.

A middle-aged Guadalupe Vallejo, nephew of rancho owner and politician General Mariano Guadalupe Vallejo, waxed nostalgically on these days in *The Century Magazine* on December 1890: "...there never was a more peaceful or happy people on the face of the earth than the Spanish, Mexican, and Indian population of Alta California before the American conquest. We were the pioneers of the Pacific coast, building towns and Missions while General Washington was carrying on the war of the Revolution, and we often talk together of the days when a few hundred large Spanish ranches and Mission tracts occupied the whole country from the Pacific to the San Joaquin. No class of American citizens is more loyal than the Spanish Californians, but we shall always be especially proud of the traditions and memories of the long pastoral age before 1840."

The sun set on the rancho era with the signing of the Treaty of Guadalupe Hidalgo on February 2, 1848, which ended the war begun two years earlier between Mexico and the United States. Mexico received $15 million; the U.S. got the territories of Texas, New Mexico, and California. The Treaty protected the land grants. However, in 1851, the U.S. Congress passed an act that required rancho owners to prove title to the new Board of California Land Commissioners. This meant money for surveyors, lawyers, and translators, and took 17 years on average. Many owners sold, lost, or were defrauded of all or portions of their land.

To accommodate her booming cattle business, Briones had bought a second rancho of 4,400 acres, Rancho La Purisma Concepcion, in 1844, near present-day Palo Alto. She kept title to it and was determined to hold on to her San Francisco rancho, Playa de Juana Briones, for her children. She fought for twelve years—all the way to the Supreme Court—and in 1856 she won.

CHRISTIAN INDIANS

Visitors sailing into the San Francisco Bay from various countries with a variety of assignments were lavishly welcomed by the priests and officers at the Presidio, and provided with horses, housing, and money. However, they were not charmed guests. While they usually penned pejorative descriptions of the Indians, visitors universally declaimed their declining numbers and the state of the mission.

Captain Otto von Kotzebue, an explorer for the Russian navy, wrote this bleak assessment: "The fate of these so called Christian Indians is not preferable to that of Negro slaves ... These unfortunate beings pass their lives in prayers, and in toiling for the monks, without possessing any property of their own. Thrice a day they are driven to church, to hear a mass in the Latin language; the rest of their time is employed in labouring in the fields and gardens with coarse, clumsy instruments and in the evening they are locked up in overcrowded barracks, which, unboarded, and without windows or beds, rather resemble cows' stalls than habitations for men. A coarse woolen shirt, which they make themselves, and then receive as a present from the missionaries, constitutes their only clothing. Such is the happiness which the Catholic religion has brought to the uncultivated Indian..."

THE LEGACY OF THE RANCHOS

Monarch the grizzly bear in the zoo at Golden Gate Park in the early 1900s.

The legacy of the ranchos can be seen today in California's orchards and irrigation system, in its place names and regional boundary lines, and in the living legends, culture, and lore of the vaquero era. "Monarch," the last grizzly bear in California, was euthanized in captivity in 1911 and handed over to a taxidermist. Now in a glass cage, he went on view in 2011 at the California Academy of Sciences in the city's Golden Gate Park. In 2012, a heritage group, The Friends of Juana Briones, lost a long fight to save her adobe house in Palo Alto from demolition. They managed to wrest away a wall, which they hope will find a new home in San Francisco or Palo Alto.

CHAPTER 3.

A GOOD HERB, A GOOD MAN, AND SAN FRANCISCO: WILLIAM LEIDESDORFF

1841–1848

Should he stay or go? It was 1841 and William Leidesdorff pondered this as he steered his trade boat from New York back home to New Orleans. He had built a business there as a shipmaster and captain and owned twelve boats. He'd left his native St. Croix and his mother, a Carib Indian with African and Spanish ancestors, and father, a sugar plantation supervisor from Denmark with Jewish ancestors, and become an American citizen in 1834. Now New Orleans had decided to enforce South Carolina's 1822 Negro Seamen Act, which effectively banned blacks from maritime jobs. To compound his woes, his beloved's family had barred him from their house, which he figured was due to his mother's racial background. He had a decision to make.

Leidesdorff sold off all his holdings, bought a schooner—the *Julia Ann*—and sailed west to Yerba Buena.

In the seven ensuing years that it was graced with his presence, Yerba Buena (translated as "good herb" and referring to the area's abundant wild mint) would lose its Spanish name and gain its permanent, American name: San Francisco. A master of many trades, Leidesdorff would play a major,

View of San Francisco in 1846-7, before the discovery of gold, showing the *USS Portsmouth* (A), City Hotel (5), the warehouse (9), and Leidesdorff's residence (11)

William Leidesdorff, 1845

though often forgotten, role in changing this place from a Mexican port town with a few roads, a dozen houses, and 200 residents to the beginnings of an American city with commercial buildings, a school, and 800 citizens.

When Leidesdorff arrived, the port—called Yerba Buena Cove—was in a slump, due to the Mexican government passing regulations limiting foreign trade. Whalers and other merchants were traveling all the way to the Sandwich Islands (Hawaii) to pick up provisions, rather than touching down in Yerba Buena. Sir George Simpson, British governor of the Hudson's Bay Company, made a round-the-world trip to size up his company's commercial future that same year. He foresaw the American takeover of San Francisco and the Hudson Bay Company retreated from doing business in the area after his tour.

On the positive side, Mexico was easing up on land grants to individuals. If you didn't marry into Mexican elite as many did, all you had to do was learn Spanish, convert to Roman Catholicism, become a Mexican citizen, and meet the price. If Leidesdorff couldn't erase the prejudice due to his skin color, he could and did convert from Lutheranism and ace the other requirements. To raise the pesos, he traveled between Alaska, Honolulu, and Mexico, trading furs, tallow, and wheat.

He bought a wharf lot in Yerba Buena and erected the town's first shipping warehouse. He also built himself a large house and was known to be "liberal, hospitable, cordial, confiding even to a fault." He also put up the first public house made of adobe and wood, which became known as the City Hotel. One and a half stories high and lacking a parlor, it had a bar, a small room for Monte (a Mexican card game), and a dining room—the largest room in town. Newspaper publisher Edward Kemble reminisced about the place in the *Sacramento Daily Union* in 1871 deeming it "the pivotal center of social life in those times."

In July 1846, the conflict that became known as the Mexican-American War was six weeks old, and the *USS Portsmouth* was anchored in Yerba Buena Bay. On July 4, Leidesdorff had the U.S. Declaration of Independence read for the first time in California from the veranda of his home. On July 9, a troop of marines from the Portsmouth rowed ashore. While the ship's band played "Yankee Doodle Dandy" in Yerba Buena plaza, they hoisted the stars and stripes for the first time in the town.

With the American takeover, the last Mexican *alcade* (mayor) declared martial law, and the plaza was re-named Portsmouth Square. Although the Treaty of Guadalupe Hidalgo officially ended the war and ceded California to the U.S. on February 2, 1848, the actions of the Portsmouth soldiers effectively ended Mexican rule in Yerba Buena.

The Americans were coming. "The Pathfinder"—Army officer John Frémont—was leading regular expeditions of "Pacific Pilgrims" to California and Oregon with scout Kit Carson by his side. On July 31, 1846, a group of 240 Mormons headed by Sam Brannan arrived on *The Brooklyn*, toting a flour mill and an outdated printing press. Brannan cranked out *The California Star*—the town's first newspaper—from an adobe windmill adjoining his house. The trickle of people arriving via overland and sea routes was gradually picking up. Piqued by drawings and rosy prose appearing in newspapers and full on promotion campaigns, Americans were making the hard slog west, resolved to create better lives.

The notion of Divine Destiny or, more familiarly, Manifest Destiny, fueled their vision and steadied their step. While never an official policy, Manifest Destiny asserted that extending American civilization westward was God's will and ordained by the nation's constitution. Underlying these ideas was a belief in the virtues of democracy and the American citizenry and in

Colonel John C. Frémont, 1856

the inferiority of Indian and Mexican culture and institutions.

On January 30, 1847, a permanent name was set when *The California Star* printed a new ordinance in both English and Spanish:

"WHEREAS, the local name of Yerba Buena, as applied to the settlement or town of San Francisco, is unknown beyond the district; and has been applied from the local name of the cove, on which the town is built: Therefore, to prevent confusion and mistakes in public documents, and that the town may have the advantage of the name given on the public map,
IT IS HEREBY ORDAINED, that the name of SAN FRANCISCO shall hereafter be used in all official communications and public documents, or records appertaining to the town.
WASHINGTON A. BARTLETT, Chief Magistrate"

Under Mexican rule, Leidesdorff was an alderman appointed by the *alcade* of Yerba Buena while serving as the U.S. vice consul to Mexico. With the American takeover, he was elected councilman and Treasurer of San Francisco. The election took place in his warehouse, an empty lemon syrup container serving as the ballot box.

With all this flurry of civic activity, it was time for a proper map of the town. Jasper O'Farrell, a civil engineer who had experience surveying ranchos, was hired. O'Farrell had his work cut out for him since the previous survey, performed in 1839 by Jean Vioget, had every street off a true right angle by 2 1/2 degrees. Maybe it was because Vioget performed the survey on horseback with chain, sextant, and compass, or maybe he sampled too much local wine. The reason for the discrepancy remains a mystery—but at least he was consistent in his error.

Until this time, the streets had no names, so O'Farrell doled out many a well-known moniker including Market, Lombard, Pine, Bartlett, and Leidesdorff; later on, a major thoroughfare was named after him. He also designated 450 lots that could be found underwater at low or high tide. Crazy? Not really. These "water lots" were considered to be valuable property for infilling.

O'Farrell ignored terrain—hills and cliffs—so that many alleys (especially in the future Chinatown) were impossible to navigate. During her visit in the

1950s, the French novelist Simone de Beauvoir observed, "San Francisco is … deliriously geometric. The blueprint seems to have been put on paper without the architect ever having seen the site. It is a drawing board with straight lines, like New York or Buffalo. The hills have simply been ignored: streets rise and fall without concern for their rigid design."

The celebration of the admission of California into the United States, October 29, 1850. The City Hotel can be seen at the other side of Portsmouth Square.

The year 1847 was filled with major accomplishments for Leidesdorff. First, he launched San Francisco's first steamboat, *The Sitka*. Second, on a meadow near the Mission Dolores, he laid out San Francisco's first racetrack. Third, he was elected chairman of the school board and donated the land for the city's first school. It was duly erected and opened on April 3, 1848, with forty pupils. Exactly a month later it closed for a day. Leidesdorff was dead at 37 years of age. The cause was "brain fever" (meningitis most likely). Flags flew at half mast around the city and on all ships in the harbor, businesses and barracks were shuttered, and the townspeople paid considerable last respects. Soldiers fired minute guns as the funeral cortege wound through the streets, arriving at Mission Dolores where Leidesdorff was buried and his stone marker can still be viewed today.

But Leidesdorff's story didn't end there. He died without a will or any relatives in California. Since California had no probate process, his estate was devalued and judged to be $50,000 in debt (around $1 million today). The city's Customs Collector and Harbor Master, Army Captain Joseph Folsom, stepped in. He traveled to St. Croix, paid Leidesdorff's mother (his father was dead) $75,000 for the rights, and sought to buy his San Francisco property. Folsom also wanted title to the 35,000 acres Leidesdorff had purchased on the American River. It was next to his friend John Sutter's property and found to be equally loaded with gold. As the case worked its way through the courts and legislature, the values of the rancho property and San Francisco harbor property ballooned. Relatives on Leidesdorff's father's side contested the will, as his family in St. Croix. In the end, Folsom's ruse worked. The properties made him one of the wealthiest men in San Francisco.

HOW THE GOLDEN GATE GOT ITS NAME

John Frémont made a series of captivating reports for the federal government of his journeys (later revealed to have been penned by his wife, Jesse Benton Frémont, and possibly others). In the July 1, 1846, entry, he recalled gazing at the strait of water between the Pacific Ocean and Yerba Buena Bay and pronouncing: "To this Gate I gave the name of 'Chrysopylae' or 'Golden Gate' for the same reasons that the harbor of Byzantium [Istanbul] was called Chrysoceras or Golden Horn."

View of San Francisco in 1850, by George Henry Burgess, 1878

CHAPTER 4.

SEEING THE ELEPHANT... AND MAYBE SOME GOLD: FORTY-NINERS AND THE GOLD RUSH

1849

You can divide the history of California into two time periods: BG (Before Gold) and AG (After Gold). A lump of gold changed the landscape, the culture, the economy—everything in the Sierra foothills, San Francisco and beyond. Gold dust had a powerful effect on people, changing some for the better, others for worse. Enter John Sutter.

An army captain in the Swiss artillery, Sutter left his country, wife, and kids (whom he brought over sixteen years later) in 1834 to avoid being tried and jailed for debts. All Sutter desired was to create an agrarian utopia he named New Helvetia (New Switzerland). By the end of 1847 he was well on his way. On the 49,000 acres he'd purchased near present-day Sacramento, Sutter was cultivating orchards, wheat and roses, grazing 13,000 cattle and 15,000 sheep, and housing a variety of employees—from farm workers to a full-time doctor. The local Indians had built him a compound containing self-sustaining businesses such as a tannery, a grist mill, and a pisco brandy distillery, as well as a jail. Surrounding all these buildings were four barricaded walls and more than 40 cannons. Sutter's Fort, as it was known, was the destination for immigrant parties, including the infamous

From left: John Sutter; Sutter's Fort, New Helvetia, 1849

Donner Party, which Sutter helped rescue from the Sierra Mountains and sheltered for months.

Perennially in debt and focusing on extending New Helvetia, Sutter decided to add a dock and lodgings on the south fork of the American River. This called for a water-powered sawmill. He hired expert James Marshall to oversee the project. On the morning of January 24, 1848, when Marshall was inspecting the previous day's excavation, he spied a shiny mineral in the water. Examining it, he exclaimed *"Eureka!"* (Greek for "I have found it!") Marshall and Sutter tested the metal: It was gold, no doubt.

Sutter tried to shush New Helvetia but the news quietly leaked out to San Francisco, where it was much debated and doubted due to the fizzling of a gold discovery near Los Angeles in 1842. But on May 12, San Franciscans saw proof. Waving a quinine bottle glittering with gold, Sam Brannan trumpeted, "Gold! Gold! Gold from the American River!" Word spread and soon a flood of men were deserting their homes and jobs and departing for the Sierra foothills, visions of mountains of gold in their heads. Indeed, to the more than 20,000 Chinese who arrived by 1852, California was Gum Shan (Gold Mountain). *The Star* newspaper ran an article that observed, "a terrible visitant we have had of late, a FEVER which has well nigh depopulated our town ... And this is the GOLD FEVER."

By the end of May, the paper ceased printing for months; staff and subscribers alike had charged off to the "diggings." For the rest of 1848, prospectors from California and Sonora, Mexico, showed up at Sutter's Fort and fanned out, unearthing more gold nuggets. When President James Polk announced the discovery to Congress on December 12 by showing off 230 ounces of gold, the news was relayed around the globe.

In 1849, the world hustled in. Dubbed forty-niners, they came from all walks of life and hailed from all corners of the United States; a third traveled from countries including France, Germany, Mexico, Chile, Great Britain, Malaysia, and Australia. Forty-niners abandoned wives, families, jobs, and crops, and cashed in savings and life insurance for the lure of wealth and adventure.

San Francisco was the entry point to the goldfields; to get there was hazardous, no matter which route the miner took. Initially, the forty-niners arrived by sea; soon there were hundreds of clipper ships lolling about in the bay, their crews off to the gold mines. Resourceful San Franciscans pulled the boats ashore, re-purposing them for rooming houses or saloons; one became the city's first jail. Many had less illustrious ends and were turned into landfill. Some ships were left to sink and rot; in 1967 while tunneling under the bay to create BART (Bay Area Rapid Transit system), engineers excavated their buried hulls.

San Francisco in 1850. The Niantic Hotel was built 1850 and destroyed in 1851.

San Francisco harbor, c. 1850, with Yerba Buena Island in the background

Once gold-seekers made it to San Francisco, they needed to stock up on provisions. They could buy from Sutter, who became a supplier when all his workers ditched New Helvetia and took up the gold pan. Sutter took a loss, but savvier businessmen, like Brannan, made 300 to 400 percent profit. Demand was high and supplies hard to keep in stock, so prices for many items surged to heights that are outlandish even today. An egg cost $1 and went as high as $4 (chickens were scarce, so most were stolen from seabird nests on the Farallon Islands, 28 miles off the bay). A hotel room garnered upwards of $150 per week, though the rats, fleas, and lice were free. The basic tool set was at least $60: gold pan $5, shovel $25, pick ax $30.

As the surface gold was harvested and deeper digging was necessary, miners teamed up to use slightly less primitive tools—rockers, cradles, and Long Toms—to wash away dirt and rocks more quickly. This placer (riverbed) mining in turn gave way to more advanced methods: sluice boxes, pressurized hoses for washing down mountainsides, and quicksilver (mercury) to magnetically attract and retain more flecks of gold. This led to dry (hard rock) mining, which proved the most lucrative of all for years to come. Dry rock mining sliced, diced, and shafted the earth using flumes, aqueducts, and tunnels. By the mid-1850s gold mining had transformed from a one-man claim to big business, with miners working underground for companies where the men at the top got rich.

Between 1849 and 1854, the U.S. Geological Survey estimates that 120 tons of gold, worth $16 billion, was pulled from the Sierras. San Francisco swelled from 812 residents in 1848 to 25,000 and growing by the end of 1849. The rapid infusion of cash and people made it California's largest, richest city.

Sutter saw his fort overrun by gold-seekers who wiped out his fields and provisions and slaughtered his livestock, destroying New Helvetia and leaving him bankrupt. He grumbled, "There is a saying that men will steal everything but a milestone and a millstone: They stole my millstone." The forty-niners called themselves Argonauts and comprised a youthful, male society—50 percent were in their 20s. (Gold Rush women were wives, boarding house managers, domestics, or "entertainers" [bar girls, prostitutes, or madams]; a few panned for gold. However with the female population less than 10 percent of the male population, it was a man's world.)

The Argonauts lived in squalid tents or boarding houses set in mud and dust in towns and camps they called Rough and Ready, Hangtown, Rich Dry Diggings, Chicken Thief Flat, Murderer's Bar, Gouge Eye, Brandy Gulch, and so on. They were comrades in work and play—drinking, gambling, and dancing together—some men cross-dressing and sleeping together—and visiting the cribs (brothels) in San Francisco. Just as often, they stole from each other and were at each other's throats; one in twelve Argonauts died, brought down by accident, disease, or murder. Racial prejudice was rampant: African Americans, whether they came as free men, escaped slaves or slaves (who were often freed), lived with limited rights and the constant threat of deportation and re-enslavement in the South; foreigners

The bar of a gambling saloon, 1855

"Seeing the Elephant," c. 1850

were driven out by a specially enacted, though short-lived, Foreign Miner's Tax; and as usual, Indians suffered the most, contending with unfair trading, land confiscation, disease, rape, and massacre.

Miners milked the mines and they themselves were milked by merchants, con artists, and dedicated criminals. The losers went home or sank to untimely deaths. The winners and optimistic survivors stayed on, emboldened to see what riches the rising city of San Francisco could offer. Win, lose, or draw, all Argonauts could say that they had "seen the elephant." Borrowed and adapted from the circus, where elephants—unseen novelties—were paraded and performed after everything else, the expression was a form of gallows humor. When a forty-niner said he'd seen the elephant, he meant that he'd seen and done it all: made the hazardous trip to the gold mines and witnessed all the hardship, chicanery, and temptations they offered.

For Sutter, the discovery of gold on his property was the beginning of a long spiral down. He lost his fort, deeded the rest of his lands to his eldest son, failed at gold mining and provisioning, and turned to liquor and law, petitioning the U.S. Congress for restitution for his wrecked utopian domain. He received some compensation but sought more, and died in his quest on June 18, 1880, in Washington, D.C. His obituary in *Harper's Weekly* on July 9 read, in part, "His claim to remembrance proved to be his great calamity, and he died, it is said, from the effect of his efforts and anxiety in importuning Congress to vote him a national indemnity because of the misfortunes he had suffered through the very discovery which has done so much toward enriching the country of his adoption."

SHANGHAIED!

To re-crew their boats, ship captains often relied on "crimps"—men who would deliver potentially renegade sailors or new ones for a fee and no questions asked. James "Shanghai" Kelly, with his fiery red hair and unkempt appearance, became notorious as the "King of the Crimps." Like other crimps—both male and female—Kelly operated out of the Barbary Coast, the city's rough, tough red-light district. He bought a boardinghouse to serve as a respectable cover.

When an order came in, Kelly had "runners" row out to the ship. The runners lured the seamen with free booze, then spirited them ashore to Kelly's place. There, he treated the seamen to liquor laced with chloral hydrate, laudanum, or opium until they passed out. The runners then stole their possessions, rolled them up naked in a blanket, rowed them out to the harbor, and hoisted them onto the ship. The captain paid the crimp fee, pulled up anchor, and the hapless sailors woke up with a helluva hangover way out at sea.

If the ship went to Shanghai, it would take the sailor a year to return to San Francisco. Thus arose the term "shanghaied," which came to be applied to anyone kidnapped and put out to sea. It was finally applied to the King of the Crimps when he himself was shanghaied.

Barbary Coast crimps

CHAPTER 5.

THE LUMBERMAN'S LAMENT: WHAT HENRY MEIGGS LEFT IN SAN FRANCISCO

1850–1854

San Francisco was a rough rock of a town ready to be polished in the early 1850s, transitioning from a place of entry and recreation for the Gold Rush hordes to a budding bona fide city that was inventing itself daily. Sperm oil streetlamps now lit the city's new planked streets and the wealth from the prosperous mines and farmlands was streaming in to support all types of business enterprises. It was a time of entrepreneurs, land speculators, and swindlers, and Henry Meiggs fit all three categories.

Meiggs was 24 when he started his career in New York City. He created a lumber company in 1835, only to be put out of business by the financial "Panic of 1837." Moving to Brooklyn, he re-established himself and became a city councilman. When the vicissitudes of the market broadsided him again, he took a new tack and began shipping lumber to the Pacific. With this venture wobbling yet again due to market capriciousness, he bought a schooner, *The Albany*, stuffed it with lumber, and in 1849 set sail for the Golden Gate. Serendipity. In San Francisco he sold the lot for twenty times what he paid. With the profits, Meiggs put up a sawmill on the bay: The California Lumber Manufacturing Company.

Henry Meiggs

San Francisco needed wood to build. And to rebuild. Six times between December 24, 1849, and June 22, 1851, fires consumed hundreds of its structures and millions of its dollars. The city rebuilt swiftly and better each time, its brash attitude expressed by one resident, "We burn down a city in a night and rebuild it in a day." Torched makeshift Gold Rush housing—tents, shanties, and reclaimed ship cabins—gave way to brick and granite and Greek and Gothic Revival style buildings. Fire-fighting methods advanced from ordinances requiring homeowners to store six buckets of water to reservoirs and a chartered volunteer fire department that had no trouble attracting members.

With so much demand for lumber, Meiggs also created a sawmill up the coast in Meiggsville (later re-named Mendocino) and began a thriving business (at last!), shipping redwood lumber to the bay. He got married, built a nice house on Telegraph Hill, and in 1850 was elected to the Town Council.

That same year, on September 9, California became the thirty-first state. In its new capital city, Sacramento, the new state government met for the first time, defying its description as "the legislature of a thousand drinks," and passing 146 laws. San Francisco got into the act, trying to curb its rowdy reputation, and enacted a law outlawing gambling on Sundays. It was widely ignored. Young men scurried past St. Mary's Cathedral on California Street with its admonishing plaque (still in place today), "Son, Observe the Time and Fly from Evil," to relish the gambling parlors and saloons nearby and visit the brothels that gave Maiden Lane its name.

San Francisco was indeed a den of iniquities, where the indecent vied with the decent, the highbrow with the low. While duels were routine and many citizens never left home unarmed, the city welcomed its first theater (an early production was titled *Seeing the Elephant*), opera, and a Philharmonic Society, which Meiggs co-founded and built a Music Hall for. Handsome and popular, Meiggs also gave liberally to folks down on their luck.

But "Honest Harry," as Meiggs was known, had a further ambition. The city possessed only one pier. It needed another one and he knew just where to put it—in North Beach, right where his depot was located. (North Beach was a real beach on the bay then, not the land filled, inland area it is today.) Meiggs wanted to enable ships, including his lumber fleet regularly arriving from Meiggsville, to easily dock and stash their goods in his warehouses.

To put his scheme into effect, he scooped up land for a song, becoming North Beach's biggest landholder. Knowing the city's players, he requested treasury funds but was voted down. Undeterred, he invested his own money to grade Stockton and Powell streets, and re-located a graveyard to extend them through the sand dunes to North Beach. He also cut a new road around Telegraph Hill, filling in the North Beach tidelands with the leftover dirt. Finally he built his masterpiece, a 2,000-foot pier that was called Meiggs Wharf (located where Fisherman's Wharf and Piers 39 and 45 stand today). To further capitalize on his huge investment and attract customers besides sailors and dock workers, he persuaded saloon owner Abe Warner to open an amusement park at the head of the wharf.

Debuting in 1856, Warner's Cobweb Palace was a happy success. Locals and tourists alike enjoyed a novel experience; visiting a pier for fun and games and dining. They could sample Dungeness crab and other seafood, check out the shops, and try the shooting gallery. Warner's saloon held the most fascination. It contained scrimshaw and other exotic bric-a-brac donated by sailors, and Warner's menagerie of exotic pets:

Francisco Street and North Beach, 1865-1867

From left: Warner's Cobweb Palace; Abe Warner inside the Palace, 1856

monkeys, bears, kangaroos, and birds. One parrot, named Grandfather Warner, cursed in four languages and accosted patrons with phrases like "I'll have a rum and gum. What'll you have?" But the main oddity was what earned the place its name: the grimy spider webs that draped behind the bar, curtaining Warner's tacky nude paintings.

Meiggs missed out on the success of the Cobweb Palace. Sales of his North Beach lots were stalled; property tax, interest bills, and street assessments were due. He was in a world of debt. What was he to do? Once again Meiggs went into action. He was aware that the mayor and city controller pre-signed warrant books for street work—blank checks, in effect, from the city treasury. Meiggs pocketed one of these warrant books, forged the necessary information, and used them to borrow money. Who wouldn't trust "Honest Harry" Meiggs?

However, there was no money in the Street Fund, so the warrants were worthless. Meiggs sunk the money into a schooner, *The American*, provisioning it with all sorts of delicacies as if preparing for a pleasure cruise. On October 6, 1854, Meiggs skimmed out through the Golden Gate, taking his family and leaving his fine house on the hill, its canaries warbling away in their cages. San Francisco reeled in his wake. Meiggs'

$1 million (approximately $28 million today) in personal debt and $800,000 in embezzled city funds wiped out hundreds of investors and twenty of the city's forty-two banks by the beginning of February.

There is an epilogue to the story, however. After a stopover in Tahiti, Meiggs landed in Valparaiso, Chile. He built railroads in Costa Rica, Chile, and Peru and made a fortune. But Harry pined for San Francisco. He wanted to come back. From his millions he paid back the city and most of his investors. Now he just had to overcome being jailed for fraud upon his return. Meiggs convinced the state legislature to pass a bill invalidating all his indictments before 1855. The governor vetoed it and Meiggs died in Lima, Peru, in 1877. But his supporters didn't give up. In 1977 a San Francisco Superior Court judge granted a motion to quash the fraud indictment against Meiggs. The judge's reasoning? Meiggs had rehabilitated himself and gone on to a higher court.

THREE OF MEIGGS' COHORTS AND HOW THEY FARED

From letf: Levi Strauss; the Boudin family; Domenico Ghirardelli

1) In 1850, a Jewish peddler from Bavaria was hawking tents made from cloth manufactured in Nimes, France, to forty-niners. With pants going for $100, a miner told him that he could really use a cheap pair. Thus "de Nimes" became anglicized to "denim" and Levi Strauss went into the jeans-making business. Or so the story goes. His company is still headquartered in San Francisco today at 1155 Battery Street, where there's a Visitor's Center and historical exhibits.

2) Isidore Boudin hit the city in 1849 along with wife and children, fresh from Burgundy, France. From a family of master bakers, Boudin set about concocting the best loaf of bread possible. Instead of using a Fleishman's yeast cake like everyone else to make his dough rise, he turned to a method dating back to the pharaohs: He used a "starter" (a fermented mixture of water, flour, and yeast), which relied on lactobacillus sanfrancisco, a local microorganism he discovered. The result? A French sourdough bread that rose to become an instant hit and become synonymous with the city. At first, Boudin delivered his loaves by horse-drawn cart. Soon he opened a bakeshop and ladies, gentleman, street sweepers—everybody—lined up. By 1854 there were 62 bakeries in addition to Boudin's.

Many a miner took bits of starter to gold fields and baked his own bread, getting the nickname Sourdough Sam. The name lives on in the mascot of the San Francisco 49ers football team. After Boudin died in 1887, his wife, Louise, ran the business, famously organizing a family bucket brigade after the 1906 earthquake to rescue the starter and use it to bake bread for the thousands left homeless. Along with other sourdough bakeries in the Bay Area, the Boudin Bakery keeps baking in San Francisco, still depending on the more than 165-year-old "mother" (original) starter to work its magic. You can see the bread baked, have a meal, and visit the Boudin museum at 160 Jefferson Street.

3) After a fleeting attempt at gold panning, Domenico Ghirardelli started a candy business in a tent in 1849. Later, he acquired a shop, only to have it destroyed by one of the great fires of 1851. But he hadn't left Rapallo, Italy, for nothing. In 1852 he imported 200 pounds of cacao beans from Peru, opened a new store, and incorporated The Ghirardelli Chocolate Company. While it's changed hands a few times and is now owned by a holding company, Ghirardelli's remains the country's second longest (after Baker's) continuously operating chocolate company. And you can still hang out at Ghirardelli Square near the bay and enjoy a steaming cup of hot chocolate elixir there.

It all goes to show that gold isn't the only way to hit pay dirt in San Francisco.

THE BARBARY COAST

From left: Barbary Coast, c. 1910; the working ladies of the Coast, c. 1890

Gambling halls, brothels, concert saloons, and bars—the Barbary Coast offered something for every illicit desire in the years following the Gold Rush. A nine-block area centered around a three block stretch of Pacific Street (now Pacific Avenue) between Montgomery and Stockton, the Barbary Coast catered to the thousands of eager Argonauts who left their families behind in search of California gold.

In San Francisco in 1849 the nearly 40,000 Argonauts who swarmed the city were met by only 700 women. Prostitution was rampant—and it was a seller's market. A seat next to a woman at a saloon could cost an ounce of gold ($16). As one Frenchman, Albert Benard de Russailh, wrote: "Nearly all these women at home were street-walkers of the cheapest sort. But out here, for only a few minutes, they ask a hundred times as much as they were used to getting in Paris. A whole night costs from $200 to $400." Gambling was equally lucrative in the gold-flushed city. It was rumored that $80,000 changed hands over a single card at a game at the El Dorado.

While the Argonauts flocked to the lawless area—along with gamblers, murders, and thieves—others in the city weren't so happy. Vigilantes cleaned it out the Barbary Coast on multiple occasions. Much of the area was destroyed by the 1906 earthquake, however. And while the attractions of the Barbary Coast rebuilt, what was once the wickedest town in the U.S. slowly became more of a tourist attraction. By the 1920s, the Barbary Coast was closed for good.

CHAPTER 6.

THE FOUNTAIN AND THE ETERNAL YOUTH: LOTTA CRABTREE

1847–1924

At 5:12 a.m. on every April 18th since 1906, elected officials, firefighters, and other San Franciscans gather at an ornate, copper-colored fountain at the intersection of Market, Geary, and Kearny. They observe a moment of silence. Then a band thumps out "San Francisco," and there are speeches and libations. All because Lotta's Fountain, as it's known, served the city's citizens on April 18, 1906, as a gathering spot for and a place for posting notices of the earthquake's dead, missing, and found.

Charlotte Mignon Crabtree—Lotta, as she was known throughout her life—was a child of the Gold Rush. She began her life in New York City in 1847, the daughter of British immigrants. Her father ran a bookstore in Manhattan but caught the gold fever and decamped to California in 1851. Two years later, her mother sold the shop and shepherded Lotta and her two brothers through the Panama isthmus to the West. They lived in San Francisco for a year, then moved to the gold mining town of Grass Valley to open a boarding house and be near her father. There, in 1855, Lotta crossed paths with a woman who would change her life.

At 34, Lola Montez, the Countess of Landsfeldt, was a performance artist with a past: past husbands, past lovers, and past lives in London, Paris, and Germany. More recently, in northern California, she'd been slammed by some bad reviews and personal troubles. She was cooling her jets in Nevada City, surrounded by a menagerie of animals, including a devoted bear she kept on a leash, when she decided to host a party for the little girls in the neighborhood.

Lotta adored Montez and loved listening to her Bavarian music box and dressing up in her costumes. Montez taught her how to sing ballads, ride a horse, smoke cigars, and, most significantly, to dance. Lotta learned to jig, fling, fandango, polka, and do a few ballet moves. One day Montez set her on an anvil in a blacksmith's shop in the mining town of Rough and Ready. Lotta tap-danced to the beat of Montez's clapping hands, delighting the small crowd.

That same year, the family moved 40 miles away to Rabbit Creek (present day La Porte). Lotta prepared for her official debut at Matt Taylor's tavern. Her mother made the girl a pint-sized costume: green frock coat and hat with boots cobbled by Taylor. While 30 percent of miners were married men, most didn't have their wives or families with them: women were scarce and children a rarity. So Lotta had a built-in audience. She also had competition on the mining camp circuit: a girls' chorus, a toddler actress, and a tot who rode bareback on a horse.

Lotta stepped on to the candlelit stage, her red-gold curls sparkling due to generous dollops of cayenne pepper. Tossing aside her shillelagh, she sang, danced, and giggled. More charm and child than talent at this point, she was an instant sensation. The men hurled money at the stage: quarters, half dollars, Mexican dollars, recently dug-up nuggets, and a $50 gold slug. Her mother scooped them into her apron and they hit the circuit.

Lotta performed on barrels and billiard tables all around gold mining country, adding soft shoe, breakdowns, and banjo to her routine, along with trick riding, impersonations, and comedy. Miners nicknamed her "La Petite Lotta," "Sparkling Ingot," "Canary Bird," "Fairy Star of the Gold Rush," and "Western Wonder." Her mother worked as her manager and accountant, making all the bookings and running her daughter's life with a firm hand.

Lotta's Fountain at Kearny and Geary streets, 1885

She replaced the apron with a leather bag and then exchanged it for a steamer trunk. When it overflowed with Lotta's earnings, she invested in real estate, bonds, and racehorses, which, over the years, paid off handsomely.

By 1856, they hit the big city: San Francisco. Lotta's repertoire now included drama and comedy. Donning dresses and pants, she acted out both female and male roles: One moment she played a fairy, the next a wild Irish boy, then a sailor with hornpipes or a lad chirping a Cockney tune. Warbling lines such as "I've a howl in my heart big enough to roll a cabbage round in," she entertained at variety halls around the city and earned the title "Miss Lotta, the San Francisco Favorite." The trunk brimmed with gold many times over but was never robbed, except by her father. Since the law stymied women's power to control their earnings at that time, Lotta made a "remittance man" out of her father, which meant she sent him a regular allowance to return to England permanently.

In 1863, at age 16, Lotta and her mother took her act on the road, touring the state and then cities including Chicago, New York, Boston, and London. The public adapted her dances, referring to them as the Lotta polka and the Lotta gallop. As she grew up, she continued to play childlike roles but added a layer of gamine eroticism and double entendres. A *New York Times* review stated that "no one could wriggle more suggestively than Lotta" and that she had the "face of a beautiful doll and the ways of a playful kitten."

The 1870s and '80s comprised her peak career years: She was the country's highest paid actress, bringing in $5,000 a week. She formed her own troupe and staged many plays including *Hearts Ease*, *Firefly*, and *The Little Difference*. As she performed in different cities, she began donating to local charities and commissioning fountains to thank her scores of fans.

In 1875, she donated the fountain that bears her name in San Francisco. Constructed of cast iron and topped by a gas lamp, Lotta's Fountain was modeled after a prop lighthouse used in *Zip*, one of her plays, and erected in the city's financial hub. At its dedication ceremony, soldiers kept a rowdy crowd at bay while the mayor praised Lotta (away on tour) and the fountain's lions' heads began spurting water into its basin.

Lotta had many admirers beyond San Francisco, including President Ulysses Grant, General William Sherman, and the Grand Duke Alexis of Russia. She "collected men like teapots," her mother once quipped. Cross-dressing offstage as well as on, she reportedly enjoyed male as well as female lovers and never married. Indeed, Attol (Lotta spelled backwards) Tryst is what she named the twenty-two-room house she built in pastoral Lake Hopatcong, New Jersey.

In 1889, Lotta suffered a fall that led to her retirement three years later. She was 45 and had been hitting the boards for 37 years. She painted, read, enjoyed her dogs and horses, and did charitable work. She came out of retirement briefly in 1915 at 65 when she traveled to San Francisco to be celebrated at her fountain and honored by Lotta Crabtree Day at the city's Panama–Pacific International Exposition.

Lotta died in Boston in 1924 at 77, leaving $4 million, most of it in charitable trusts to WWI disabled vets and their dependents, animals, needy actors, convicts, hospitals, and graduates of Massachusetts Agricultural College. Seven of the eight original trusts are thriving today, worth approximately $8 million. Her obituary in *The New York Times* assessed her as "an eternal child." While she was much more than that both offstage and on, certainly her fountain—now a restored national landmark—is an eternal part of San Francisco.

ENTERTAINING SAN FRANCISCO

In her scant 39 years, Lola Montez (born Eliza Gilbert in Ireland) fashioned a life for herself and gained a reputation that both scandalized and titillated people. While short on talent and skirt, she tantalized male audiences the world over with her bawdy spider dance, during which she shook spiders created out of cork, rubber, and whalebone from her costume and stomped them dead.

Lola Montez, 1851

On Christmas Eve 1910, the city was rewarded for its rebuilding efforts after the earthquake by the appearance of world-renowned Italian opera singer Luisa Tetrazzini. "I never thought I would be a street singer but I want to do this for San Francisco, because this is the first place in the United States where I sang, and because I like San Francisco," she said. "San Francisco is my country." A throng of 90,000 to 250,000 (press estimates vary) swarmed Lotta's Fountain. Cable cars, streetcars, horses, and horseless carriages halted. Tetrazzini stepped forward on the platform. Bedecked in a rhinestone-studded gown, ostrich-plumed hat, and rose-colored wrap, she belted out Christmas carols and ballads. Her rapt audience joined in for the finale—"Auld Lang Syne." A plaque on Lotta's Fountain commemorates the event.

Luisa Tetrazzini, 1912

CHAPTER 7.

THE EMPEROR HAD BOTH CLOTHES AND LOYAL SUBJECTS: JOSHUA NORTON

1819–1880

"On the reeking pavement, in the darkness of a moonless night under the dripping rain, and surrounded by a hastily gathered crowd of wondering strangers, Norton I, by the grace of God, Emperor of the United States and Protector of Mexico, departed this life."

Thus read the front-page obituary of Joshua Norton—known by one and all as Emperor Norton—on January 9, 1880, in the *San Francisco Chronicle*. Rumors had it that Napoleonic blood ran through Emperor Norton's veins and that his penniless appearance was a hoarder's cover for extreme wealth. Wasn't it true that since returning to the city in 1859 he had issued a series of royal proclamations, patents and bonds? While no one took these decrees seriously, everyone wondered what would the police find when they examined Norton's lodgings on Commercial Street.

Joshua Abraham Norton was born around 1819 in England to Jewish parents who re-located to South Africa when he was a toddler. In 1849, with $40,000 in his pocket from his father's will, Norton left Capetown to try his luck in San Francisco. Parlaying his money into real estate in North Beach, he

profited to the tune of $250,000 (around $7.5 million today). In 1853, China suspended rice exports, sending local prices zooming from 4 cents per pound to 36 cents per pound. Perceiving an opportunity to increase his fortune, Norton laid out $25,000, paying a rate of 12.5 cents per pound for a cargo ship of rice embarking from Peru. By the time his ship came in, others had arrived and the price for a pound of rice had dropped to 3 cents. Norton tried to void the contract, and failing, took the matter to court. When the battle finally concluded in 1857, he was defeated and bankrupt.

Norton vanished. Two years later, he returned, a different man. On September 17, 1859, he sent an announcement to the city's newspapers decreeing himself Emperor of the United States.

The city didn't accept his emperor status right away; respect grew with time, persistence, and familiarity. From his throne—an old armchair in his Imperial Residence on Commercial Street, where he paid 50 cents in daily rent for a small room on the third floor with other distinctly non-royal furnishings— Emperor Norton issued all manner of proclamations. He dissolved the Republic and ordered the army to clear the halls of Congress, reasoning that "...the universal suffrage, as now existing through the Union, is abused; that fraud and corruption prevent a fair and proper expression of the public voice; that open violation of the laws are constantly occurring, caused by mobs, parties, factions and undue influence of political sects..."

Norton also issued his own money in the form of signed promissory notes that ranged in value from 50 cents to $10. As his subjects grew to know and love him, they gleefully accepted these ornate bills imprinted with his seal and picture. In fact many looked forward to seeing Emperor Norton wending his royal way about town, dressed in his regal attire. His crown was a black beaver top hat with a rosette and a white ostrich plume. His boots, made of practical, durable leather, were slit to accommodate his ever-growing corns. His robe—fit for a commander-in-chief—consisted of a light blue army officer's frock coat and was festooned with gold epaulettes and buttons and a cavalry sword. After considerable wearing, when the uniform's ragged appearance seemed to mock His Royal Highness and the militia, the city supervisors would step in and present His Highness with a new uniform. For this deed, Emperor Norton granted a "patent of nobility in perpetuity" to each supervisor.

As news of Emperor Norton's sovereignty spread around the bay and across the country, San Franciscans and visitors alike delighted in sighting their ever-accessible monarch. They bowed or curtseyed and

Emperor Norton's $10 bill, 1879

exchanged their dollars for his signed currency. They also bought souvenirs from vendors: Emperor Norton Imperial cigars, postcards, pennants, plaster statues, and the like. The Emperor was good for business and business in turn was good to him. He ate for free all over town and merchants were happy to pay him a small "tax" or fulfill a request in return for a placard professing his patronage. Signs popped up in store windows all over town boasting, "By Appointment to His Majesty, the Emperor," "Royal Printer to Emperor Norton I," and "Gentlemen's Outfitters to His Imperial Majesty."

The Emperor was definitely a man about town, especially on Montgomery, then a waterfront street. Routinely, he made royal inspections to ensure his subjects' safety. He examined public works, marketplaces, and wharves. He envisioned future projects, calling for a transportation tunnel beneath the bay, (foreseeing an important artery of today's BART [Bay Area Rapid Transit] system) and conceiving a suspension bridge from Oakland to SF (anticipating the Bay Bridge). In 1939, E Clampus Vitus—an organization dedicated to preserving the American West—acknowledged the Emperor's prescience by placing a plaque on the bridge.

Emperor Norton put forth three other proclamations that reflect the kind of society he believed his subjects were owed. First, he commanded communities worldwide to send delegates to a Bible Convention in San Francisco, "towards the obliteration of all religious sects and the establishment of a Universal Religion." The emperor himself attended all churches and temples, refusing a state religion in support of citizens' religious rights. Second, he commanded that Leland Stanford, an owner of the Central Pacific Railroad, should "grant us possession and save the trouble of legal proceedings." Third, he forbade the use of a word that San Franciscans today still welcome as much as an earthquake or reference to

A cartoon by Edward Jump shows Bummer and Lazarus begging for scraps from Emperor Norton

Rice-A-Roni: "Whoever after due and proper warning shall be heard to utter the abominable word 'Frisco,' which has no linguistic or other warrant, shall be deemed guilty of a High Misdemeanor, and shall pay into the Imperial Treasury as penalty the sum of twenty-five dollars."

Norton withstood threats to his rule with characteristic kingly aplomb. The most serious occurred one morning when he was reading the newspaper in the sumptuous Palace Hotel. A manager mistook him for a pauper and summoned the police. Officer Armand Barbier proceeded to haul Norton to the city dungeon, where he spent the night. Luckily, a jail beat reporter noticed Norton in the precinct log; the news went viral, *The Evening Bulletin* relaying it thusly:

"In what can only be described as the most dastardly of errors, Joshua A. Norton was arrested today. He is being held on the ludicrous charge of 'Lunacy'. Known and loved by all true San Franciscans as Emperor Norton, this kindly Monarch of Montgomery Street is less a lunatic than those who have engineered these trumped up charges...The blot on the record of San Francisco must be removed."

The next morning a hooting, hollering crowd swarmed the jail. Police Chief Patrick Crowley reportedly appeared and made this statement:"On behalf of the San Francisco Police Department, I have offered Emperor Norton our official apology... There is no official reason to question his sanity, and statements from concerned citizens like all of you have proven that. It has also been sufficiently proven that he is recognized and appreciated as our Emperor. Therefore, from this day forward, I am instructing all police officers of the City of San Francisco to salute the Emperor whenever appropriate."

The emperor pardoned Barbier and enjoyed being saluted by officers from that day forward.

The tale of Emperor Norton cannot be fully told without mention of his two canine consorts. In the days of Norton I, San Franciscans had no use for dogs and poisoned or otherwise caused their untimely demise ... unless they could catch rats. Such a pair of hounds was Bummer and Lazarus, known to have polished off eighty-five of the vermin in twenty minutes on one occasion. Rovers of the streets like Emperor Norton, they became associated with him in the press, especially in the cartoons of Edward Jump, much to his royal displeasure.

Sadly, as all sovereigns and subjects alike must, Emperor Norton's reign came to an end. While passing St. Mary's Church on the way to an evening lecture at the California Academy of Sciences on January 8, 1880, he succumbed to a stroke before a summoned carriage could arrive. The front-page headline in the *San Francisco Chronicle* announced "Le Roi est Mort" (The King is Dead).

Ten thousand of his reverent subjects viewed his remains at the undertaker's parlor at 16 O'Farrell Street. Another 30,000 stood solemnly as his funeral cortege meandered through two miles of city streets. Then they celebrated with street parties all over the city. An examination by the police of his room on Commercial Street turned up little of monetary value: spare change, a stock certificate worth 98 shares in a defunct gold mine, an assortment of hats and walking sticks, and a bogus telegram from Czar Alexander II congratulating the emperor on his marriage to Queen Victoria.

MARK TWAIN MEETS TOM SAWYER

Mark Twain, who knew, liked, and respected Emperor Norton and wrote about him as well as his dogs, lived in San Francisco from 1861 to '63. Twain spent his time carousing—invariably broke and writing for various newspapers to pay his tabs—and hanging out with E Clampus Vitus, an irreverent fraternal order born of the Gold Rush given to commemorating brothels, saloons, and other historic places overlooked by historical societies. Twain's primary friend and drinking buddy was a former steamboat engineer (like himself), firefighter, and saloon-keeper named Tom Sawyer. Yes, though Twain's time in San Francisco was short, it helped him create his most memorable character.

CHAPTER 8.

A WOMAN OF SMARTNESS AND SCANDAL: MARY ELLEN PLEASANT

1814–1904

Mary Ellen Pleasant amassed a fortune, cross dressed to free slaves, and defied the conventions of her day. She was a woman of mystery, as accounts of her life differ and not all the facts are clear. She was born in 1814 by her own telling, in 1817 by others', and in 1812 as chiseled on her tombstone. In her book, *Memoirs and Autobiography*, she states she was born in Philadelphia to a Kanaka (Hawaiian) father and Louisianan mother. But biographers and historians aren't sure; she may have started life in Georgia, the daughter of a slave and a white plantation owner. What is fact is that by 6 years old Pleasant was living on Nantucket with the Husseys, a family of white abolitionist Quakers.

While Pleasant received no formal education, she grew up in a liberal society of freed blacks and anti-slavery whites under the wing of Mary Hussey. Pleasant worked as a clerk at Hussey's dry goods store and was an ace at accounting, describing herself as "a girl of smartness." She gained business savvy, assertiveness, and the ability to read and influence people. "I have let books alone and studied men and women," Pleasant reflected. "I have always noticed that when I have anything to say people listen. They never go to sleep on me."

As a young woman, Pleasant moved to Boston, where she worked in a tailor's shop, earned money as a church soloist, and married James Smith. He was mixed race and well off—a carpenter, a contractor, and the owner of a plantation in Virginia worked by free slaves. Smith was also an abolitionist and he and Pleasant were active conductors (escorts) on the Underground Railroad, guiding slaves on tracks (routes) from Virginia to the Promised Land (Canada).

When Smith died in 1844, he left Pleasant between $15,000 and $50,000 (accounts differ, but the sum made her wealthy), to carry on their work. She did. This resulted in a price on her head so she skipped west. As Frederick Douglass contended in his newspaper, *The North Star*, "the wealth of California ... should be, shared by colored as well as white men."

Pleasant arrived in San Francisco around 1849 with a new husband, free man John Pleasants (later shortened to Pleasant), a ship's cook who was often away at sea. The Pleasants entered a society with 464 blacks, where domestic services garnered a premium. Pleasant touted her services as a personal chef, starting a bidding war that garnered her the princely wage of $500 per month. She also opened one lucrative laundry after another.

Along with many blacks in San Francisco and elsewhere, Pleasant worked for a living and for civil rights. Blacks attended church together, put out a newspaper, *The Mirror of the Times*, and created the Franchise League political action group. She helped fund and found the San Francisco Athenaeum Institute, a saloon and meeting place that housed an 800-book library on the second floor. One of her employees remarked, "The Negroes were timid but not nearly as unthinking as many imagined. Sharp thinkers like Mammy [Pleasant's unfortunate moniker] ... formed an organization to protect them."

The Pleasants, and other members of the black community continually aided and harbored fugitive slaves and fought the state's racially discriminatory laws such as its Fugitive Slave Act. She and her husband traveled to Canada, as participants in and donators to abolitionist John Brown's plot to incite a slave rebellion in the South. With rebellion in mind, they bought land in Ontario so the newly freed slaves could settle there. "I then went back to the United States and secured a trusted man to go with me along the Roanoke River and incite an uprising of the slaves," she wrote in her memoir. "I was dressed in the clothes of a jockey and he had horses along, and we posed as people connected with the turf." And how did the slaves respond? "They were very much taken with the idea of participating in a fight for their own freedom," Pleasant recounted.

The Last Moments of John Brown (detail), by Thomas Hovenden, 1882-1884, Metropolitan Museum of Art

When Brown started the rebellion at Harper's Ferry before Pleasant and others had laid all the necessary groundwork with the slaves, Pleasant was astounded "that the affair upon which I had staked my money and built so much hope was a fiasco." Brown was hanged and Pleasant feared the same fate because his captors found a note from her in his pocket: "The axe is laid at the root of the tree. When the first blow is struck there will be more money to help." Her clumsy handwriting saved her, as detectives read her "MEP" as "WEP." Pleasant remained proud of her association with Brown. At her request her tombstone in Napa is engraved, "She was a friend of John Brown's."

Returning to San Francisco in 1861, where blacks now totaled more than 1,000 (out of approximately 68,000 residents), Pleasant began cooking and housekeeping for the town's white elite, such as the Woolworths. She had already been investing in gold, silver, and quicksilver, but now she got insider business tips from her employers. She enlisted Lisette Woolworth's help when she took another daring action for civil rights in 1866.

In that era, streetcars were wagons drawn by horses or mules. Even though the majority of white patrons didn't object, the railroad company's policy was to eject black passengers or not stop for them. One afternoon, when

Side view of "Mr. Bell's mansion," 1926

Pleasant tried to take the streetcar with Woolworth, the conductor refused to let her board. She sued the company and both she and Woolworth testified. In 1867, the court ruled in Pleasant's favor, awarding her $500 in damages. Although the damages were later reduced to $0, the case set a precedent for awarding damages that was revived in the 1950s and '60s civil rights era. The 1870s proved a busy and lucrative decade for Pleasant as she built a fortune estimated at $1 million to become the city's "wealthiest colored person" according to the *Oakland Enquirer*. She opened opulent boardinghouses that catered to the needs and whims of the city's top gentlemen.

She also made a financial partnership with William Bell, a bank vice president. He moved into her lavish Octavia Street Italianate mansion. She fronted as his housekeeper while actually investing their and her own money in a variety of ventures. Soon the place was referred to as "The House of Mystery" or "Mr. Bell's mansion," though she held title. The rumors of what went on there swirled around the town and frequently into the press, even when Bell married and his children lived there. The public had no doubt that "Mammy Pleasant" was more than a housekeeper, but could only speculate as to her true role as she careened around town in her fancy carriage and plain straw bonnet, living a life unfathomable for a woman, especially a black one.

The next two decades saw Pleasant ensnared in scandal, bleeding money, losing her health, and caught up in public court battles. In 1883, out of principle and friendship, she testified for the ravishing Sarah Althea Hill, who sued the wealthy former senator William Sharon for divorce and alimony after he took on multiple mistresses. He denied the marriage, swearing that she was just another mistress.

The case was sensationalized from coast to coast, damning all three of them with its trumped-up tawdry details. The defense accused Pleasant of "baby farming" because she had clandestinely found homes for several unwanted babies. It also forced her to reveal the amounts of her holdings and alleged that she controlled Hill by being her madam and practicing voodoo on her.

Sarah Althea Hill, between 1880 and 1887

Sharon died a month before the verdict went in his favor in 1885. Hill married one of her lawyers. He assaulted the judge (a crony of Sharon's) who had ruled against her and was shot by the judge's bodyguard in 1889, spiraling Hill into insanity.

But Pleasant's trials were far from over. An ailing Bell died from an accidental fall in the mansion in 1892 and the rumors had it that "Mammy pushed him." His son, and later his wife, Teresa Bell, decided to wrest control from Pleasant, suing her for the house, properties, and other monies. In her 80s, she fought back, saying, "I'd rather be a corpse than a coward." Again she was vilified in the press, and eventually Bell forced her out of the mansion. (Today six of the many eucalyptus trees she planted—all that remains of the property, which burnt down in 1925 and was replaced by a hospital—are preserved as Mary Ellen Pleasant Memorial Park.)

Pleasant moved to a lesser property and, when terminally ill, friends took her in. She died in 1904. Pleasant was remembered in the local paper for her philanthropy and claimed in her memoirs not to care about public opinion. "If a write-up about me put a blanket on somebody's bed or gave a household meat and bread, I would let them lay my character down in the middle of the road and let the whole world jump on it and turn it over and let them go it again."

CHAPTER 9.

AN IRON HORSE AND AN OCTOPUS: THE BIG FOUR CREATE A RAILROAD EMPIRE

1859–1869

Engineer Theodore Judah had a plan and a problem. The West Coast was isolated from the East Coast; he wanted to unite them and accomplish the engineering feat of an age: a transcontinental railroad. He'd already mapped the arduous Sierra part of the route and laid the West Coast's first line, The Sacramento Valley Railroad, which ran from Sacramento to Folsom. Now he needed investors. He'd lobbied for federal funds and beseeched San Francisco's big pockets to no avail.

One night in 1859, Judah found himself meeting above a mining supply store in Sacramento with some new prospects: Mark Hopkins, Jr. and Collis P. Huntington (co-owners of the store), a lawyer and a grocer named Leland Stanford, and Charles Crocker, owner of a dry goods store. These self-made, moderately successful WASP businessmen—"The Associates," as they called themselves, "The Big Four," as they came to be known—would put up the dough: $15,800 apiece (approximately $329,000 in today's dollars). The five of them incorporated as the Central Pacific Railroad of California.

On July 1, 1862, President Abraham Lincoln signed the Pacific Railroad Act, greenlighting the transcontinental railroad. Unluckily for Judah, the Big Four were in it purely for profit and empire building. As they began to rook the government, which had loosed some subsidy funds, Judah journeyed east to raise capital to buy out their shares and regain power. More unluckily for him, he contracted yellow fever in Panama and died at 37 in New York in 1863.

Theodore Judah, 1866

Barely shedding a tear, the Big Four went into gear. They took over Judah's lobbying tasks, twisted legislators and elections (Stanford was elected governor in 1861), and crushed competition to create construction companies and control waterfronts in Oakland and San Francisco—all in preparation for the cross country railroad and its connecting lines.

To build the railroad, their Central Pacific Railroad Company went head to head, literally, with the Union Pacific Railroad. The government was doling out a $16,000 bond for each mile of track laid, and the race was on to reach the finish line at Promontory Point, Utah. The Big Four divvied up the work: Huntington hunkered down in the east to funnel railroad cars and equipment west via The Horn of South America and bribe congressmen in Washington, D.C.; Stanford covered the political bases; Hopkins took the role of treasurer and record keeper; Crocker oversaw construction of the railroad; and all of them wangled funds and manipulated connections every tie of the way.

As the Union Pacific team raced west, stocked with Irish laborers, and, increasingly, Civil War veterans, Crocker was determined keep labor costs low. His Irish laborers took no guff, frequently threatened to strike, and often left for the gold mines. Crocker turned to a readily available, underutilized workforce at the time commonly considered "the dregs of Asia:" the Chinese. Countering prejudice and doubts in their abilities, Crocker hired 50 Chinese laborers for one day. This test proved so successful that he employed some 20,000 Chinese, importing thousands

Hopkins (left) and Stanford mansions, 1887

In early April 1906, with all of the Big Four ensconced in grandiose mausoleums, their Nob Hill manors burnt to the ground with great fires that swept the city after the earthquake.

CHAPTER 10.

TAKING A RIDE ON THE ROPE: ANDREW HALLIDIE AND SAN FRANCISCO'S SLOT MACHINES

1873

Horse manure littered the streets of San Francisco in the wake of horsecars. But worse, these horse-drawn streetcars of the 1860s caused horrifying accidents; their everyday operations sent many a horse to an early grave. Andrew Hallidie, 33, witnessed the problems and reported to the Mechanics' Institute, a group he helped found, "I was largely induced to think over the matter from seeing the difficulty and pain the horse experienced in hauling cars up Jackson Street from Kearny to Stockton Street, on which street four or five horses were needed for the purpose—the driving being accompanied by the free use of the whip and voice and occasionally by the horses falling and being dragged down the hill on their sides by the car loaded with passengers sliding on its track."

Hallidie was just the engineer for the job. In 1852, he had made the trek to California from England with his father, who owned a share in a gold mine. When it flopped the next year, the senior Hallidie went home. The son, Andrew, remained, supporting himself as a surveyor, blacksmith, and designer of suspension bridges, still hoping to strike it rich by gold mining on the side. He found his riches in another vein in 1856, when he took a

From left: Andrew Hallidie; Hallidie's suspension bridge in Nevada City, Calif., c. 1880

consulting job. The problem? The hemp rope used to pull skips loaded with ore from the mines across the countryside to the mills regularly wore out every two and a half months. Hallidie devised a machine to make wire rope, which his father had invented. The new rope lasted two years.

With his eyes open to opportunity, Hallidie started the California Wire Rope and Cable Company in 1857, and manufactured wire rope without competitors for many years. He depended on the rope to construct more bridges in the mining West. He also employed it to construct an aerial tramway referred to as the "Hallidie Ropeway." In 1867, he took out the first of a series of patents, patenting his suspension bridge, his wire rope, and the Ropeway.

All the while, gold was turning into silver. After the discovery of silver mines in Nevada in 1859, profits were starting to be reaped from this new metal, which would soon bring more wealth to San Francisco than the Gold Rush. Four Irish-American partners—James Fair and John Mackay (miners) and James Flood and William O'Brien (stockbrokers and former saloon owners)—established the Consolidated Virginia Mining Company in 1871 in San Francisco. They operated silver mines and sold stock in them; initial shares went for $4 to $5, skyrocketing to $710 (around $12,000 today) as mining and drilling methods tapped more ore and the "silver rush" reached fever pitch. In 1873, a shaft sunk more than 1,200 feet into the Comstock Lode hit the "big bonanza"—netting $1.5 million a month for the investors. Fair, Mackay, Flood, and O'Brien became known as the "Bonanza Kings" and brought more wealth to San Francisco. (Flood's Nob Hill mansion—its exterior to be precise—survived the 1906 earthquake and fires due to his insistence on building it out of sandstone. The Pacific Union Club, a closed-mouth conservative men's club, has owned and occupied it ever since.)

Hallidie's company furnished the Comstock with wire rope and his Ropeways, but his mind was still turning. If ore cars could run on his wire rope, why not some kind of horseless streetcar?

In 1870, Benjamin Brooks, a lawyer, proposed a cable railway and the city granted him and his three partners a franchise to build one in. They were unable to raise the necessary capital as San Franciscans were too busy sinking their money into underground silver to consider an over-ground mechanical car conquering their notoriously hilly streets. Hallidie purchased the plans and franchise. After persuading his friends from the Mechanics' Institute to invest and the Savings and Loan Society to lend $30,000, he went to work.

San Franciscans took notice when long slots began to be slashed into their streets. The genius of Hallidie's cable car system was that it ran at 9.5 mph on continuously moving cables supported by grooved wheels stationed underneath in the slot, or channel, in the street. A cable barn housed the giant sheaves (pulleys) that turned the cables for the different car lines. The cars were fashioned from remodeled horsecars. To stop a car, a gripman released a grip from the cable and squeezed a brake. (You can see and hear the sheaves and learn lots more about the history of cable cars and the gripmen and women who operated them at the free Cable Car Museum right at the Mason stop on the Powell Street line on Nob Hill.)

Finally the day came when the cables were up and running, the sheaves pulling, and the test car set in the slot, ready to take on the 2,800-foot Clay Street

The first cable car, starting at Clay and Jones streets on Nob Hill in 1873

Cable car climbing Clay Street Hill, August 2, 1873.

Hill (Nob Hill). It was August 2, 1873, at 5 a.m.—Hallidie picked the time the fewest people would be on the streets. The San Francisco Municipal Railway recorded what happened next, "Only a handful of people climbed out of their beds to watch a small group of men anxiously tinkering as the first cable car in history made its maiden run that day..."

Positioned in the car at the grip wheel, the gripman reportedly peered down the steep hill cloaked with fog and promptly bolted. Hallidie stepped forward and took the wheel himself and began to turn it.

"The car slowly 'took the rope' and rolled smoothly over the brink and down the 20 percent grade at an even nine miles an hour," the report continued. "Thus was set in operation the first cable line in the United State, the Clay Street Hill Railroad."

A month later, after more tinkering and testing, the first public cars clanged out. The public was only too glad to take a "Ride on the Rope" instead of huffing and puffing up its hills. By 1890, with the city's population near 300,000, there were ten different lines, each with a stable of distinctly colored open-air cars, for a total of 600 cars traversing more than 100 miles of track and employing 1,500 people, many of them former horsecar drivers. San Francisco's slot machines (as revered newspaper columnist Herb Caen dubbed them in the 1940s) were a success, making Hallidie a wealthy man. They also changed the city, allowing neighborhoods to spring up on previously inaccessible hills and valleys. Nob Hill wouldn't have become Nob Hill without them. Railroad tycoons Leland Stanford and Mark Hopkins bought their own cable car lines to carry them to their mansion gates.

In 1892, the first electric streetcar chugged through the streets. Soon streetcars were cutting into cable car territory, replacing them on flat surface routes. The 1906 earthquake wiped out a half dozen or so more cable car lines, which were also replaced by streetcars. By 1912, the "Muni" (the San Francisco Municipal Railway, the county's public transit system) appeared, eventually eroding both streetcar and cable car territory.

A bigger blow came in 1947, when Mayor Roger Lapham, in his annual speech to the Board of Supervisors, pronounced "the city should get rid of its cable cars as soon as possible." While acknowledging that there were "strong sentimental reasons for keeping this old, ingenious and novel method of transportation," he argued against them. "The fact remains that the sentimentalists do not have to pay the bills and do not have to run the risk of being charged with criminal negligence in the very possible event a cable breaks and a car gets loose on one of our steep hills."

These were fighting words for socialite Friedel Klussmann. She spoke at convocation of twenty-seven women's civic groups and formed the Citizen's Committee to Save the Cable Cars.

From left: Friedel Klussmann; a demonstration to save the cable cars, 1954

Cable car decending Clay Street Hill

The group started a petition drive to allow voters to amend the city charter and compel the city to run the cable lines. The mayor and his allies on the Public Utilities Commission pulled out all the stops to combat Klussmann and the Committee, claiming the cars were unsafe, unprofitable (the fare was 7 cents), and that young men showed no interest in "pulling grips" as gripmen retired. The cable crusaders countered that cable cars were cheaper to run than buses and safer—in fifty-four years of operation not a single cable had broken.

Letters flooded in from across the country and around the world in favor of saving the cable cars. The value of the tourist dollar was not lost on either party, or the public. In November, Measure 10 to save the existing five lines of cable cars passed by a 3 to 1 margin. The battle wasn't over: In 1954, the Committee lost a round and the number of lines was cut to three, which still run today. In 1964, San Francisco's cable car system was declared a national landmark. Supreme Court Chief Justice Earl Warren delivered the chief speech at the official ceremony:

"There is affection for San Francisco's cable cars in many lands. ... I associate them, as hundreds of people do, with stimulating experiences, superb views of the Bay and the sheer excitement of being in 'everyone's favorite city.'"

The most fitting tribute to Hallidie, Klussmann, columnist Caen, and all the rest who toiled to keep the cars gliding through their well-oiled slots appeared in a *San Francisco Chronicle* article the following day:

"The San Francisco cable car, invented out of necessity arising from the city's steep and frequent hills, has now climbed to the peak of esteem and respectability. The perky, noisy, woefully archaic little contraption is now the revered symbol of a metropolitan city, but has attained national recognition—and protection—as a national monument. This obsolete, creaking, inadequate, slow, expensive-to-operate, money-losing—and uniquely San Franciscan—piece of the last century machinery has risen in the world like a Horatio Alger hero and is now a tourist attraction that brings thousands of visitors and millions of dollars to this community annually."

THE CABLE CARS' LEGACY

Hallidie died in 1900. In 1917, the esteemed architect Willis Polk designed a multi-story office fronted by a glass curtain two feet from the building, the first of its kind in the U.S. Named the Halladie Building as a posthumous honor, it still stands at 130 Sutter Street near Union Square.

When Klussmann died in 1986 at age 90, the *Los Angeles Times* obituary noted, "She left no immediate survivors except, of course, the 37 cars that continue to wend their way up and down the city's hilly, 113-year-old system at 9 m.p.h." That day the cars were curtained in black. Later, the turnaround at the terminal of the Powell-Hyde Line at the bay gate was dedicated to her.

CHAPTER 11.

OH MR. SANDMAN, BUILD ME A PARK: JOHN MCLAREN

1870s

"Me boy, if ye have nothing to do, go plant a tree and it will grow while ye sleep."

–Scotsman Donald McLaren to his wee son John McLaren

San Francisco grew from 56,802 in 1860 to 149,473 in 1870, becoming the United States' tenth largest city—and growing. It was time for a grand urban park. The mayor and Board of Supervisors spent the latter half of the 1860s acquiring the land (an amount more than double the acreage of New York's Central Park) and drawing up plans. On April 4, 1870, the Board passed an act ordering that, "the land ... extending from Stanyan Street of the East to the Pacific Ocean is hereby designated and shall be known as the 'Golden Gate Park.'"

However, there was a huge obstacle to realizing an emerald swath of crowd-pleasing greenery: sand. The land set aside for the park had not been developed or much occupied before for a good reason: Its 1,017 acres were covered with hills of sand that were often blowing in the wind. Dubbing the site "Sand Francisco," skeptics judged the park an unachievable dream.

From top: Sand hills at the future location of Golden Gate Park, 1865; Ocean Beach after 1903

John McLaren, 1927

The Sonoma Democrat opined that, "Of all the white elephants the city of San Francisco ever owned, they now have the largest in Golden Gate Park, a dreary waste of shifting sand hills where a blade of grass cannot be raised without four posts to keep it from blowing away."

The Board hired Scottish horticulturist John McLaren as Superintendant to tackle the problem. Before accepting the job, McLaren got the Board to sign-off on two conditions: 1) A $30,000 annual budget for grading and planting along with all the water he desired; and 2) Weekly deliveries of dung and other organic street sweepings (horseless vehicles were still years from dominance).

McLaren combined the street sweepings with branches, soil, and clippings to create a rich concoction that he mixed into the sand. His predecessor, the park's original creator, engineer William Hammond Hall, had tried to tame the sand by planting lupine. It failed to take hold. Next up was barley, which died after a few months. Calling on his experience working the soil on Scotland's Firth of Forth, McLaren sowed sea bent grass. It took.

Simultaneously, McLaren initiated a long-term project to contain the swirls of sand formed daily at Ocean Beach by wind and waves. He erected a barricade of branches and twigs backed by a lath fence 100 feet from the shoreline. Forty years later, he witnessed the result: The waves sculpted a berm 20 feet high and 300 yards wide, neatly blocking the sand from spreading over the Great Highway, which runs along the coast. His berm still holds today.

When it came to planting trees, McLaren put in fir, pine, redwood, eucalyptus, and other varieties, growing many of them in the park's nursery.

In 1875, the park boasted 60,000 trees; by 1890 there were 155,000. To keep water flowing to all the new flora, the newly formed Park Commission drilled three wells. By 1910, one sent 1.5 million gallons of water daily to a reservoir tucked into Strawberry Hill. Two more pumped 75,000 gallons per hour into the park, propelled by two giant, Dutch-style windmills.

McLaren sunk lakes where there were none, put in paths and roads, and planted groves and gardens. As he continued to mold the park, residents began to take notice. In 1873, 15,000 people visited it and were enchanted by its walkways, benches, streams, meadows, flowers, and grottoes.

Hall and McLaren believed in creating a natural park, an oasis from urban dwelling that, in Hall's words, was "not a catch-all for almost anything which misguided people may wish up it." McLaren forced the Board to agree that the park would never display any "Keep off the grass" signs. He fought the addition of any monuments or statues—which he termed "stookies"—in the park. If he lost the battle and a stookie was installed, he quickly obscured it with shrubs or trees. This applied to a statue of himself, which he hid away in the stables for years. Unearthed after his death in 1943, it stands today in the John McLaren Rhododendron Dell.

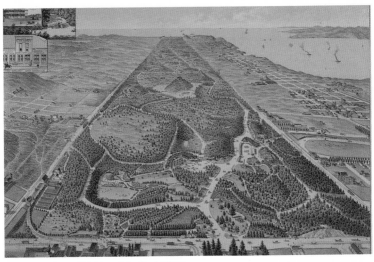

Bird's-eye view of Golden Gate Park, 1892

Working from dawn to dusk, out of the office as much as possible, McLaren was the patriarch of the park, revered by the public as "Uncle John," reviled by politicians, and feared but respected by his employees. He resisted commercialism, allowing concessions only at Stow Lake (boat rentals) and the Japanese Tea Garden (tea). He (and others) opposed the California Midwinter Fair of 1894, which brought 2.5 million visitors and a handsome profit. He was glad to help tear down the fair's temporary buildings along with its plantings after its January to July tenure.

The 1880s and 1890s brought droves of bicyclists in bloomers, split skirts (shocking!), and knickerbockers, making the neighborhood desirable. The park was world-class and helped inspire San Francisco's new nickname: "Paris of the West."

The cable cars and streetcars that regularly stopped at the park increased its popularity. McLaren resisted these too. He did not want the San Francisco Railway Company running a line through his park, complaining, "You'll ruin the trees." The company countered that the map showed no trees where its proposed line would go. "Then your maps are wrong," he retorted. "That's where the rhododendrons are." An inspection was set for the next morning.

Japanese Tea Garden, 1898

Sure enough, when the railway's engineers showed up, they found a thicket of rhododendrons. McLaren's army of gardeners had planted them the night before. Outwitted, the railway dropped the project.

McLaren felt the same way about cars, believing they frightened the bicyclists and the horses. Cars were banned in various parts of the park and are restricted to this day, especially on the

Conservatory of Flowers, c. 1897

weekends. He also took on the police department. When the chief asked to remove a tree that was too close to the local station, McLaren replied, "I'm a reasonable man, let's compromise, and you move the station." Later, he donated park land for a police station. It was a win-win gesture: The new building scotched city plans to send Sunset Boulevard through the park to Lincoln Park.

Just as trees and shrubs were established in the park, so were buildings. They materialized the dreams and the desires of San Franciscans in the Victorian era, revealing a belief in progress and an eye toward Europe with an array of architectural styles, like the Conservatory of Flowers, the Temple of Music (the band shell in the music concourse), the Academy of Sciences, and the de Young Museum (the latter two featuring modern additions). McLaren himself lived in the park in a Spanish Colonial Revival house built in 1896. Now called McLaren Lodge, it's the headquarters of the Recreation and Parks Department.

For a while antelope, elk, bison, bears, goats, sheep, deer, geese, and more ranged the park. Most were remanded to a zoo constructed in their honor (today's Fleishacker Zoo). The handful of bison left today reside in a paddock in the park.

Music Pavilion, Golden Gate Park, c. 1902

In 1917, McLaren turned 70, the mandatory retirement age for a park superintendent. Rather than lose him, the Board of Supervisors wrote a special law that doubled his salary (in lieu of a pension) and granted him lifelong tenancy. In 1927, McLaren Park was dedicated to him. Located in a southeast part of town, its 318 acres of open space make it the city's second largest park. It contains few concessions and no stookies. When McLaren died in 1943, at age 96, after managing the park for 56 years, his body went on view in the rotunda at City Hall. His funeral procession took him through his beloved Golden Gate Park one last time.

Since it was created, the park has been a vital part of the city. On January 14, 1967, the Human Be-In took place in the park's stadium. Timothy Leary famously urged the 30,000 young people grazing in the grass to "tune in, turn on, and drop out." In 2001, Warren Hellman put on the first Hardly Strictly Bluegrass Festival, an ongoing crowd-pleaser.

Each year 19 million people traipse the park. There's a favorite spot for weddings (the Garden of Shakespeare's Flowers); for smoking pot (Hippie Hill near the Janis Joplin tree); and for remembering (the AIDS Memorial Grove).

Visitors and residents alike have benefitted from McLaren's vision and life's work—he planted more than 2 million trees during his lifetime—but he would brook no praise. Rather he'd say, "Work and life in a good garden were the nicest things I could think of as a boy and I've not changed my mind."

Egyptian Hall at Memorial Museum, 1894

CHAPTER 12.

THE SHANGHAI ORPHAN WHO FOUGHT BACK: MARY TAPE

1885

"If John Chinaman don't leave here, we will drive him and his supporters into the sea!"
–Denis Kearney, founder of the Workingmen's Party, speaking at a sandlot rally, 1877

"Is it a disgrace to be Born Chinese? Didn't God make us all!!!"
–Letter to the San Francisco Board of Education from Mary Tape, April 8, 1885

In 1857, an abandoned baby girl was placed in an orphanage close to Shanghai. When she was 11, she came to San Francisco, either brought by missionaries or as a *mui tsai*, (indentured servant in Cantonese). No one would have predicted that she would live a middle class life outside of Chinatown, let alone fight a trailblazing battle for education.

In 1868, Chinese females made up 5 percent of the Chinese population, which numbered more than 11,000 out of the 135,000-plus people in the city. With its population and economy continuing to soar, San Francisco stabilized socially, creating permanent institutions and organizations.

Excluded from this society and restricted to Chinatown, the Chinese formed associations and institutions to take care of themselves: to settle disputes and to provide social welfare, education, and medical care. The men worked in banking, retail, manufacturing, fishing, and publishing, dominating the city's laundry business (since the Gold Rush, when there were few women and no other men would do wash), laboring on the railroads, and working in vice businesses (opium, gambling, and prostitution). The women had far fewer opportunities; around 75 percent were prostitutes. Most had been kidnapped or sold as mui tsai by destitute parents who believed that their daughters would be married to suitable husbands once their years of servitude were up. Sometimes this happened, but ordinarily the girl was forced into brothel work in Chinatown. Either way—prostitute or mui tsai—they were disdained as "slave girls" by non-Chinese.

A slave girl in holiday attire, Chinatown, 1896-1906

The abandoned girl never talked of her past; never divulged her Chinese name. In 1868, she was taken under the wing of a Reverend Augustus Loomis and lived outside of Chinatown. Christians were actively proselytizing Chinese and starting to rescue girls from prostitution in Chinatown to train them to be good Christian wives. Reverend Loomis determined the best place for the girl: an orphanage run by the Ladies' Protection and Relief Society in an Italianate mansion in a sparsely populated area on a hill.

There she was named Mary McGladery, after the matron of the place. Mary was the only Chinese girl among 175. She learned to read and speak English, paint, and play piano—to dress, think, and act like a middle-class American. In 1875, at 18, she met Jeu Dip, a 23-year-old émigré who'd taken the name Joseph Tape. Like many men from China in San Francisco, he'd left Tiu Shek Chuen (Skipping Stone Village) in Canton to better his lot in the U.S. Since dialects differed among the California Chinese, the couple communicated in English. Reverend Loomis married them at the First

Cigar-making in Chinatown, c. 1878

Presbyterian Church and the newlyweds moved to Cow Hollow (the area west of Van Ness and Lombard streets), then occupied by middle-class non-Chinese. Mamie Tape was born in 1876, the first of their four children.

By 1870, San Francisco's Chinese numbered 11,728, making them 7.8 percent of the city's rapidly rising population. That same year the city enacted the first of many exclusionary laws, this one seeking to stop Chinese and other "Asiatic" prostitutes from immigrating. Aligning with the "anti-coolie" anti-Chinese immigrant movement, the U.S. Congress passed the Page Act in 1875, which barred not only Chinese prostitutes but also Chinese contract laborers and criminals. Compounding these woes, 1876 brought an economic depression and unemployment that many Caucasians blamed on "John Chinaman," who they believed had conspired with the fat-cat bosses to undercut wages.

A successful drayman (wagon hauler of goods) and Irish immigrant named Denis Kearney founded the Workingmen's Party in 1877 to do something about it. Kearney went to the sandlots (now occupied by the main public library) near City Hall and gave speeches that always ended with "The Chinese must go." Warning of "bullets over the ballot" if official measures weren't taken, Kearney whipped up the crowds and helped incite a series of repressive actions against the Chinese. Tradesmen, mechanics and craft guilds (cigar makers, shoemakers, and others) unleashed economic boycotts to eject Chinese from manufacturing jobs and pressed consumers to buy products "made by white labor." Gangs of 20 to 150 men took to the streets, beating, stoning, spitting on, and lynching Chinese, torching their homes and businesses.

From Left: Dennis Kearney; a meeting of the Workingmen's Party on the Sandlots

These rampages culminated in the "Sandlot Riots" of July 1877. The police—who normally kept hands off Chinatown except for opium raids—showed up to defend a battened down Chinatown. Bent on burning up the steamships that brought in Chinese, the mob was beaten back by police and firefighters, and only succeeded in gutting the lumberyard next to the arrival dock. As a drayman, Joseph Tape made daily runs in his wagon to pick up newly arrived Chinese at the dock and deliver them to their first residences. What he encountered from Kearney's rabble is unknown.

In 1879, Kearney's henchman, Ira Kolloch, was elected mayor. Many opposed him and the anti-Chinese movement, especially Charles de Young, editor of the *San Francisco Chronicle*. After de Young denounced the mayor repeatedly, Kolloch's son shot him dead, was tried, and exonerated. In 1882, the anti-Chinese movement found its biggest victory when the Chinese Exclusion Act was passed by the U.S. Congress, to severely curtail immigration from China.

In addition to his drayman work, Joseph Tape bonded Chinese sailors (to guarantee they wouldn't jump ship), was an interpreter, and owned a telegraph express office. Mary learned to operate the telegraph so they could communicate throughout the day when he was away at work.

Until 1884, their two eldest children were tutored at home. That year, Mamie turned 8 and the Tapes decided it was time for her to go to a real primary school. The options were: the missionary school in Chinatown or Spring Valley School. (Founded in 1852, Spring Valley was the first public school in the state and was attended by Lotta Crabtree and Cyril Magnin.) In 1880,

California's legislature had passed a law entitling all children to a public education. Yet Mamie was one of a thousand Chinese children that the San Francisco Board of Education was determined to keep out. Agreeing with the exclusionary position of the state superintendant of schools, the board had promised to dismiss any principal who admitted a "Mongolian" child and vowed to fend off the "invasion of Mongolian barbarism."

The First Blow at the Chinese Question, from the *The San Francisco Illustrated Wasp*, 1877

Mary and Joseph walked Mamie over to the Spring Valley School. Principal Jennie Hurley, a Canadian immigrant of Irish parents, turned them away at the door. Mary and Joseph sued. In January 1885, in the matter of Tape vs. Hurley, the Superior Court decided in favor of the Tapes. In his ruling, the judge noted that Chinese paid school taxes and cited the equal protection clause of the Fourteenth Amendment. "To deny a child, born of Chinese parents in this state, entrance to the public schools would be a violation of the law of the state and the Constitution of the United States," the judge said. Further, he ruled that the law allowing schools to reject students with "filthy and vicious habits" was intended to be applied to individuals, not ethnic groups. The school board appealed. In March the state Supreme Court upheld the judge's ruling.

Anticipating this outcome, the board had prepared a two-pronged counterattack. When the Tapes and their counsel knocked on the school door, Principal Hurley stopped them once again. She claimed that Mamie's vaccination was dated too late and that the child's class was already filled with sixty children. Hurley referred them to the new school that the Board had created for Chinese only.

Mary went home and wrote a scathing letter to the board in imperfect, but perfectly clear, English:

"I see that you are going to make all sorts of excuses to keep my child out off the Public schools. Dear sirs... You have expended a lot of Public money foolishly, all because of one poor little Child...

May you Mr. Moulder [school superintendent], never be persecuted like the ways you have persecuted little Mamie Tape...I will let the world see sir What justice there is When it is govern by the Race prejudice men!...I guess she is a more of a American then a good many of you that is going to prewent her being Educated."

Five days later, with no other recourse, Mary sent Mamie and her brother Frank off in one of Joseph's wagons to the new Chinese school. White reporters were on hand. Expecting the Tapes to dress in traditional Chinese outfits and Frank's hair to be in a braided queue, one newsman observed that the Tapes wore Western garb and hairstyles. Another wrote that Mamie was probably the "most intelligent member of the class."

Mamie and Frank learned Cantonese from their schoolmates—four boys from the Missionary school—who dressed traditionally and wore their hair in queues. From its small start the school grew over time to include more students. (In the 1920s the Chinese students were allowed into integrated schools but it took the 1954 Supreme Court decision of Brown vs. the Board of Education to put a legal end to segregated schools everywhere.)

In 1895, the Tapes crossed the bay to Berkeley, most likely to purchase a house where they pleased, since San Francisco prohibited Chinese from buying property outside of Chinatown. Mamie had children who attended integrated schools; her son was first in the family to go to college. In the 1960s Mamie recounted her experience to her great grandchildren, "They said all the 'pigtails' would be coming," but my parents "fought like heck."

A Chinese man carrying supplies, c. 1880

CHAPTER 13.

BOOKS, BATHS, AND BEYOND: THE LEGACY OF ADOLPH SUTRO

1830–1898

It's reported that seals barked a funeral dirge as the body was carried away from its fog-wrapped estate overlooking the Golden Gate. It seems that the seals (actually sea lions) appreciated Adolph Sutro more than the people of San Francisco when he passed, but with time that has changed.

Sutro was born in 1830, in German-speaking Prussia. His mother moved the family to Baltimore in 1850, following her husband's death. Sutro skipped on to the Golden State where he started several businesses with cousins in Stockton, then in San Francisco, and did respectably well. But his training and heart were in engineering: He delighted in rigging a five-foot wood figure with a pump so that it smoked a pipe and lured customers into one of his two tobacco shops. Sutro moved on to tinkering with a chemist on a method to extract silver from mine tailings. While he experimented, his family grew and his wife supported them by opening and running two boarding houses.

The payoff came in 1861, when he established a small mill—Sutro Metallurgical Works—near Virginia City, Nevada, and refined more silver

Adolph Heinrich Joseph Sutro

from the tailings than the original mining had produced. Soon he was processing six tons of tailings a day to the tune of $10,000 (around $250,000 today) in net proceeds a month. Within two years, he owned a much larger mill and an assay office. Leaving his brother Charles in charge, Sutro poured his energy into his next brainstorm: a mine tunnel.

Conditions at the Comstock mines in Nevada ranged from barely tolerable to fatal. Tens of thousands of men worked the bowels of the earth, hundreds of feet down, where they combated lethal gasses, floods, and temperatures as high as 140 degrees. Eyewitness Mark Twain observed in his usual acerbic style, "Sometimes men fall down a shaft, there, a thousand feet deep. In such cases the usual plan is to hold an inquest."

Sutro proposed drilling a four-mile tunnel 1,650 feet deep in the mountain to drain the deadly water build-up from mining operations. Combined with shafts he'd puncture for ventilation, the tunnel would drastically improve working conditions and enable gravity to aid ore cars in extracting silver more efficiently. It was a terrific plan in terms of safety and profitability. Unfortunately, he was up against mine speculators and owners—William Ralston and William Sharon of the Bank of California and "the Octopus," the multi-industry empire controlled by the "Big Four" railroad tycoons. Determined to continue selling mine shares and siphon off all the profit, they viewed his project, and the fees they'd need to pay him, as a threat. Tagging the tunnel Sutro's Folly, they barred potential lenders in the West from giving Sutro the necessary start-up funds.

Sutro managed to do a little excavating and obtain some funds, but the Bank of California threw up a roadblock in the form of a federal bill to block Sutro's way. Congressman William Kelley of Pennsylvania addressed the congressional committee on mines and mining: "I propose to speak for the miners, 45 percent of whom die in the vigor of their young manhood, prostrated by the heat and poisoned by the atmosphere in these mines.

These industrious men ... swarm behind Mr. Sutro and beg Congress to vest all the rights in him that will enable him to reduce for them the terrible doom to which the Bank of California would condemn them."

The bill died, but was just one of a string of wins and losses for Sutro as he fought a bitter battle against Ralston, Sharon, and the Octopus for nine years.

In 1869, an explosion in Virginia City's Yellow Jacket mine claimed forty-five lives that Sutro's Folly would have saved. Miners themselves put up the necessary funds and Sutro began construction on his tunnel. Author Samuel Dickson recalled the first day of construction in the book *Tales of San Francisco*, "...in a pouring rain the miners and their families came marching down the hills and out of the streets of Virginia City ... Before them, in a three-seater buggy, clad in a Prince Albert and a white beaver hat, rode Sutro. Bands played and ... great tables were heaped with barbecued pork and beef, and loaves of bread, and twenty kegs of beer ... A cannon fired a salute. Sutro flung aside his black coat, rolled up his sleeves, tossed his white hat into the road, and shouldered a pick."

Sutro led the miners and frequently labored side-by-side with them, facing off mudslides, cave-ins, and avalanches while building the tunnel and sinking the shafts. The miners trusted Sutro. He paid them $3 per hour, a dollar less than the going rate, but gave them stock options ($1 per day payable upon completion of the project) in his company, Sutro Tunnel. Still, they faced treacherous conditions.

The deeper the crew dug into the earth, the more they had to stop and wait for the foul-smelling, boiling river to drain out the mouth of the tunnel. The day finally came to blast a major connection between a shaft and the tunnel at the Savage Mine inside Mount Davidson.

The entrance to the Sutro Tunnel in the late 1800s

Sutro maintained that cool air would flow upwards. Experts pooh-poohed this. The miners drilled eight holes on one side of the mine walls. Stationed below on the other side, Sutro sealed them. The miners then stuffed eight Rigorret powder cartridges into the holes and lit them. The blast rocked the mountain, propelling smoke and hot air up the tunnel with such force that it knocked the miners out. Once the dust and debris settled, the miners struggled to their feet and flung a rope ladder down to Sutro who climbed up.

The $6.5 million tunnel was a breakthrough, both literally and figuratively. However, the years of delay due to fighting Ralston, Sharon, and the Octopus took their toll. The tunnel was overdue and would soon be obsolete. Sutro realized that the Germans were manufacturing better water pumps and that mines were being dug deeper. He unloaded his stock, making $5 million, and returned to San Francisco in 1879.

Sutro's next folly, as many city dwellers saw it, was sinking his fortune into what were considered the city's sandy, worthless "outside lands." He acquired one twelfth of the city's land, and began planting eucalyptus saplings into his sand lands, creating Sutro Forest on what he named Mount Parnassus—what's been called, officially for years now, Mount Sutro. (Today UCSF and the city own different parts of Mount Sutro and Sutro Forest, which offer the public a garden, hiking, and wildlife. Sutro Tower, the red-and-white broadcast tower that dominates the western cityscape, is planted on an adjacent lower hill.)

In addition, Sutro began creating public buildings that San Franciscans and visitors alike are mad about to this day. Inspired by a tide pool, he designed and installed a public aquarium near Cliff House, a bar and restaurant that he owned. Cliff House burned twice during his ownership and twice he rebuilt it, the second time erecting a grand, seven-story Victorian edifice. Dubbed the Gingerbread Palace by critics, it burned in 1907 and its replacement—today's Cliff House—still stands.

For himself, Sutro spent more than $1 million transforming a cottage overlooking the ocean into a modest (for the times) estate. Traveling around the world, he scooped up books for a personal library that, at 300,000 volumes, was one of the most extensive in the U.S. His estate also contained

From left: Sutro Railroad in 1897; Sutro Baths and Cliff House

plaster imitations of ancient statues, a conservatory, a wooden tower, and all the expected accoutrements of the Gilded Age: urns, gardens, gates, and promenades. He opened the grounds, dubbed Sutro Heights, to visitors at no charge. He built a railroad to get there, endearing himself to the public by charging lower fares than the Octopus's lines—no small feat.

In 1894, Sutro ran for mayor against the machine with the motto "Down with the Octopus," expecting to lose. The anti-corruption theme of his campaign was being sounded from San Francisco to New York. Sutro won, beating Nob Hill's candidate and becoming the city's first Jewish mayor. Politics exasperated him, however, and his two-year term did not live up to its promise. He was relieved to leave office and appraised his performance candidly, "I have always been master of a situation; I have always had a number of men under my employ, and they did as I told them. I could not manage politicians."

The last great contribution Sutro made to San Francisco was completed two years before he died. He spent $1 million on Sutro Baths, a Victorian entertainment complex resembling a classic Greek temple, which he gifted to the city. For 25 cents, patrons could dip in a freshwater pool or any of six salt water pools. They could also watch the bathers from a special gallery, stroll terraces of exotic plants, delve into two museums (art and natural history), tuck in to the restaurant, with seating for 1,000, or take in a play or concert. The place accommodated thousands, and thousands showed up. In ruins today, the Sutro Baths live on in their posters, which show bathers in Victorian-age bathing costumes, an entrancing reminder of what was.

The Sutro Baths, 1921

Descending into dementia, Sutro died in 1898 at 68, leaving much land and many a donation in his wake. Over time, San Franciscans grew to appreciate Sutro for what he left behind. From Cliff House you can still see the water-filled ruins of Sutro Baths as they shimmer near the ever-crashing waves of the Pacific.

A snapshot of Cliff House, with a woman identified as "Little Miss Pierson" on the beach

CHAPTER 14.

EARTH, WIND, AND FIRE: LEONIE VON ZESCH AND THE GREAT EARTHQUAKE

1906

The evening of April 17, 1906, Italian tenor Enrico Caruso was singing at the Opera House in Carmen, enrapturing San Francisco's diamond- and pearl-encrusted upper echelon. Several blocks away, in the house she shared with her mother, 23-year-old dentist Leonie von Zesch prepared for her next day's work. She focused on the "grass-green dress and the jaunty little hat with flower-covered bandeau" to add zing to her day. Little did she realize that the day would bring a major zing—measured at 7.9 magnitude—of its own.

In the 1840s and early 1850s, San Francisco had survived the devastation of six manmade fires. From 1860 to 1905 the city had been jostled by earthquakes of varying magnitudes, but on April 18, 1906, the city experienced a one-two punch that almost knocked it out. First, preceded by an intense, rolling foreshock of twenty to twenty-five seconds, the Big Quake hit at 5:12 a.m. Trailed by a long series of strong aftershocks, it lasted forty-two seconds and has been recorded as a 7.9 magnitude. (Seismologists can only estimate its magnitude because the temblor agitated seismograph styluses so violently that they veered off the recording paper.) Second, fifty-two fires pumped by easterly winds socked the city, causing nearly

The San Francisco Fire on Sacramento Street, April 18, 1906

90 percent of the day's damage. Earth, wind, and fire: They produced a cataclysm of man and nature that all but obliterated the city, rendering it a smoking ruin.

In her autobiography, von Zesch describes that morning:

"Simultaneously Mother and I cried, 'Earthquake!' I crooked my knees to put my feet on the floor, but before my toes had touched the carpet, my head was back on the pillow. The house rocked violently and I rocked with it, unable to uncrook my knees or straighten my spine. ... there was an unforgettable humming, grinding sound that not even the walls shut out, the grinding and breaking of myriad things all over the city."

All over the city buildings had fallen, teetered, or broken apart, and gas lines had ruptured—28,000 in total. The new $5.7 million City Hall collapsed, partially due to faulty concrete, like quite a few other buildings. Landfill areas, notably in the Mission, liquefied, taking out rows of houses. Telegraph, telephone, and electric lines snapped. Bulls, horses, and other livestock ran wild on the streets. Chemicals, sewage, and other noxious, potentially lethal, substances spilled out. Worst of all, three hundred water distribution mains and 23,200 connecting pipes shattered, a few fire stations were crushed, and the fire chief, sleeping on the third floor of the fire station, plunged down three floors and was seriously injured. (He died four days later, repeating his oft-made pleas for an auxiliary salt-water system, never conscious of the fires engulfing the city around him.)

Von Zesch and her mother emerged from their room to inspect their home: "Except for two loose bricks on one of our chimneys, we could see no damage to the structure of our house ... Diagonally across from us, on the corner of Leavenworth Street, was the Granada, a showy hotel decked with prism-glass chandeliers and much brass ... It had broken in half. The front now lay on the sidewalk, exposing a tier of rooms ... an ornate brass bedstead ... stood on the very edge of what was left of a third story chamber floor, with a puffy satin comforter hanging negligently from it."

Von Zesch and her mother finally came down to earth enough to feel hunger pangs, only to encounter a gas company official who told them not to light their stove because it could ignite escaping gas. The stove warning—handed down from Mayor Eugene Schmitz—was too late. Already, people were cooking breakfast on their gas stoves; one woman on Hayes Street wiped out her neighborhood with what was dubbed the "ham and eggs fire."

Firefighters—numbering 584 with 41,000 feet of wrecked hose—did what they could with their horse-drawn equipment and the help of residents. Stopped by the lack of water, they used every source of liquid they could muster: abandoned wells, sewer water, soda water, barrels of vinegar. They soaked burlap bags with wine to swat out flames on Telegraph Hill. Battling alongside the servants the wealthy had left behind, they tried to save the mansions on Nob Hill but had to retreat due to the heat.

The fires were out of control.

A trio of officials conferred to manage the situation: Mayor Schmitz, ineffectual in part because of suspicion of graft (for which he would be convicted a little over a year later); ex-mayor and future senator James Phelan, who took charge; and Army General Frederick Funston, stationed at the Presidio, who brought in the troops. Funston assumed command when the interim fire chief—desperate without water—came up with what

View of Market Street toward the ferry, 1906

was to prove a disastrous decision: To dynamite buildings in order to create firebreaks. "Owners of buildings, tears streaming down their faces, consented to the dynamiting for the good of the cause," von Zesch recalled. "Others refused; their buildings went anyway."

The army ferried explosives across the bay, and its captains supervised the detonations. Employing gunpowder (which proved combustible) as well as dynamite, the blasts set more fires than they stopped. Temperatures reached 2,000 degrees in places. San Franciscans were on the move: More than 250,000 (out of a population of 400,000) were homeless. The refugees fanned out around the city, dragging trunks, boxes, furniture, and pets, piling possessions on baby buggies, go carts, and other wheeled vehicles— heaving them all up and down hills to dodge the flames.

They rested on their trunks, camping on the streets, then in tents at the Presidio (20,000 people), Golden Gate Park (40,000 people), Alamo Square, Portsmouth Square, and a hundred other makeshift refugee camps in other unharmed parks and squares. Later, many migrated to sturdier temporary cottages or made their own crude shacks. More than 100,000 people escaped the city: Some headed south in carriages, others north across the bay in boats. (The parents of Mayor Joseph Alioto [1968–76] met while being rowed away from the city.) A panicked, nearly naked Caruso fled his suite at the Palace Hotel for New York, swearing never to return to San Francisco. He never did.

Walking the crowded streets, von Zesch and her mother were at times lifted off their feet and carried along by the dense horde. There was hysteria, there was gratitude for being alive, and, von Zesch recalled, "All barriers of race and creed, color and social station were let down. In a way it was like a picnic of some vast fraternal organization."

As the catastrophe expanded, the mood changed. Although historians record there was little looting by residents, fear was rampant. Funston blockaded the harbor (to confiscate food from ships) and sent his army to patrol the streets; Mayor Schmitz ordered the army and police to close all liquor stores and authorized them in writing "...to KILL any and all persons found engaged in Looting or in the Commission of Any Other Crime."

Time and calamity took a terrible toll. People became dazed, crazed, catatonic, or demoralized. Some drank liquor as it ran down the streets after the military dumped over barrels. "Mind and body can bear the extreme of excitement for a comparatively short time only," von Zesch observed, "after that the most terrifying experiences become commonplace."

A change in the winds— from the unusual easterly to the usual westerly direction—helped the fire burn itself out, and after seventy-two hours rains finally came: The conflagration was over. It wiped out Chinatown, Union Square, Nob Hill,

Home life among the refugees: a street of tents in the Presidio, 1906

Leonie von Meusebach-Zesch, 1902

the financial district, the poor area "south of the slot" (Market Street), the Mission district, the "den of iniquity" known as the Barbary Coast—more than 80 percent of the city. The damage amounted to more than $500 million (more than $13 billion). The official death count was held at 379, a ridiculous figure since blacks, Chinese, Japanese, Italians, Native Americans, and poor whites weren't counted. Additionally, the total was underreported to stimulate real estate prices and punch up the rebuild effort. The actual total is considered to be upwards of 3,000.

Fire consumed von Zesch's office and her and her mother's rental house and home. They had time to pack a suitcase of clothes and other basic items. Von Zesch hopped a hay wagon with the suitcase packed and her mother walked to the Presidio where they joined the relief effort. Von Zesch worked as a U.S. army dental surgeon in a tent and her mother documented survivors for the Red Cross. San Francisco began to rebuild immediately, determined that the city would go on, bigger and stronger than ever.

Von Zesch moved on to perform dentistry with a variety of people in distant places: Mormons and Hopi Indians in Arizona, and gold miners and Inuits in Alaska. Later in life she typed out her autobiography on thousands of sheets of onion-skin paper, trying to get them published but not succeeding before her death in 1944. Decades later her niece discovered the manuscript in her attic and published it as *Leonie: A Woman Ahead of Her Time* in 2011.

In the book, von Zesch reflects: "The earthquake and fire marked a turning point in many lives. As always with disaster, for some they proved a springboard to better things; for others they meant irreparable ruin. But in one way or another, everyone had a chance to start anew."

A group of earthquake refugees sitting outside of a decorated tent called the "House of Mirth" with signs indicating an available elevator and running water, 1906

CHAPTER 15.

A BANKER, A BEDMAKER, AND BOHEMIANS: A.P. GIANNINI AND THE EARTHQUAKE AFTERMATH

1906–1949

I saw thee in thine anguish tortured! prone!
Rent with the earth-throes, garmented in fire!
Each wound upon thy breast upon my own,
Sad City of my grief and my desire.

Gray wind-blown ashes, broken, toppling wall
And ruined hearth—are these thy funeral pyre?
Black desolation covering as a pall—
Is this the end—my love and my desire?

Nay! Strong, undaunted, thoughtless of despaire,
The will that builded thee shall build again,
And all thy broken promise spring more fair,
Thou mighty mother of as mighty men.

Thou wilt arise, invincible! supreme!
The world to voice thy glory never tire;
And song, unborn, shall chant no nobler theme—
Great City of my faith and my desire.

Ruins of the Bank of Italy building destroyed in the earthquake, April 19, 1906

–Excerpt from "San Francisco: April 18, 1906" by Ina Coolbrith, California's first Poet Laureate, written the day of the quake after abandoning her home to fire.

As thousands of San Franciscans streamed south out of the city the day of the 1906 earthquake, 35-year-old A.P. (Amadeo Pietro) Giannini left his home in San Mateo and headed north into the city. Normally the 17-mile trip would have taken 30 minutes on the train, but the tracks were a tangled mess so he walked and hitchhiked. At noon he reached the Bank of Italy, which he'd founded in 1904, in North Beach. It was intact and open (thanks to two employees) but Giannini was astute. "At the rate the fire was spreading," he figured, "no place in San Francisco could be a safe storage spot for the money."

Requisitioning two wagons from his stepfather, owner of the city's biggest wholesale produce company, Giannini packed up all the bank's records, along with as much furniture and supplies as he could fit. He added mattresses and crates of oranges—and $80,000 (about $2 million today) worth of gold and silver, which he hid underneath everything. After stowing the load at his brother-in-law's for the night, the two returned to San Mateo with the two employees. Secreting the dough in Giannini's chimney—crushed by the quake—they took turns guarding it.

The following day, Giannini was back in the city. His bank was demolished as he'd foreseen, along with 80 percent of the city. The bigger banks, such as Wells Fargo, couldn't get into the vaults of their immolated buildings for two weeks until they cooled down. (Opening a still-warm vault would trigger spontaneous combustion of any untouched contents.) So the other banks—their buildings ruined—re-opened with limited services only. Fearing a run on banks after the disaster, California's governor had declared a 30-day bank holiday. Giannini ignored this. He had a history of bucking the establishment and succeeding. Plunking a bag of gold atop a wooden plank straddled over two barrels, he re-opened his bank with unlimited services.

The oldest child of Italian immigrants, at 7 Giannini saw his father—a fruit and vegetable farmer—shot and killed by an employee over a $1 pay dispute. At 14, he went to work in his stepfather's produce business and became a partner. They did so well that, bored at age 31, he sold his half to the employees and retired. The next year, Columbus Savings and Loan Society—a medium-sized bank in North Beach, San Francisco's Italian district—asked him to join its board. He accepted but soon fell out with the directors. Banks at that time were institutions by and for the upper class. Giannini aimed to lend to the "little fellows," working and middle-class men and women.

He found a saloon in North Beach and converted it to a bank, keeping the bartender on as an assistant teller. Borrowing $150,000 from his stepfather and ten friends, he opened his own lending institution, the Bank of Italy, in 1904. To attract business, he took to the streets and went door-to-door, educating the

A.P. Giannini with his family aboard *SS Giulio Cesare*, 1923

populace on how a bank operates and on the benefits of making deposits and obtaining loans. This solicitation, something unheard of in those days, mortified his fellow bankers who dismissed him as a "huckster seeking customers in much the same way as he had once sold pears and apples."

In addition to Italians, Giannini lent to Chinese, Mexicans, Portuguese, Russians, and other immigrants. Customers deposited more than $700,000 (around $14 million today) in Bank of Italy during its first year. By March 31, 1906, the bank's loans—almost entirely in real estate—outpaced deposits by $200,000. Less than three weeks later, due to the quake and the aftershocks, dynamiting, and fires that followed, most customers' property was gone. Giannini wanted to stay in business and help people rebuild their homes and businesses so, he used his "plank office" and his brother's unscathed house on Van Ness to make loans based on a handshake and a person's character, not on the assets they owned.

The "upbuilding," as the reconstruction of San Francisco was termed, had started in earnest across the city while rubble was still being cleared. More than 1,000 bricklayers were working away to fix chimneys so people could cook safely. Even as people were still numb from the shock of loss,

Removing debris at Third, Kearney, and Market streets, c. 1906

Three years after the quake, San Francisco, April 1909

signs began sprouting up in the smoldering rubble, "On this site will be erected a six-story office building to be ready for occupancy in the fall." New overhead electric streetcar lines were strung up, replacing smashed, outdated cable car lines. City officials attempted to relocate Chinese and other disrespected minorities to the outskirts of town but failed. Chinatown was rebuilt, as were fresh dens of inequity in the Barbary Coast area.

Giannini called upon ship captains and lent them money to travel to Oregon and Washington. "Get all the lumber you can," he instructed them. "It will soon be in greater demand than anything else." He also built the New California Hotel to frugally house the 6,000 Italians and others immigrants rolling in to upbuild the city.

Giannini was proud that his customers repaid all their earthquake loans. He continued to make loans to people and industries that other banks wouldn't. A partial list includes the wine industry and other agricultural ventures, Disney and the film industry (when they were considered low class and high risk); much later he provided start-up cash to Bill Hewlett and David Packard. Giannini added more branches to his bank, and in 1930 changed its name to Bank of America. He made loans to fund construction of the Golden Gate Bridge and continued to change the way banking was done, impacting home and auto loans, installment credit plans, and holding company structures. He founded his own holding company, Transamerica Corporation, in 1928. By 1945, Bank of America was the world's largest non-government bank, and was aiding postwar re-construction in Italy and other parts of Europe.

Bank of America victory bond ad, 1943

Although he influenced banking nationwide and globally and amassed a colossal set of companies, Giannini himself was not enthralled by money. He died in 1949 with $500,000 (about $4.75 million today) in assets, claiming that, "Money itch is a bad thing. I never had that trouble." Thousands of common people lined the streets and 2,500 jammed into St. Mary's Cathedral the day of his funeral service. All Bank of America branches were closed. The city and citizens he had helped rebirth were thriving.

Murphy bed, 1916

In 1900, William Murphy lived downtown on Bush Street near Burritt, where the partner of Sam Spade (Dashiell Hammett's fictional private eye) would be plugged by Brigid O'Shaughnessy in *The Maltese Falcon*. Two dames were causing Murphy a headache: his girlfriend and his landlady. His bed dominated the space in his studio apartment, so to have a woman over—day or night—was considered indecent and would get him evicted. What to do? He had an idea. Grabbing some old door parts—a jamb and hinges—he fashioned them into a pivot and bolted them to the wall.

Soon he had it: a disappearing bed that popped out of the wall and retracted as desired. He married the girl and borrowed money from her father to patent his "Murphy In-A-Dor Bed" and start his company. His pull-down beds proved popular in San Francisco apartments and elsewhere, making Murphy's Wall Bed Company a success. Unfortunately many a folding bed snapped shut during the earthquake, causing multiple deaths due to suffocation or broken necks. Still, they were often installed in new apartments built after the quake.

Near the financial district and Union Square, near the corner of Post and Taylor streets, sits a six-story, vine-covered brick building: the headquarters of the Bohemian Club. Engraved on a plaque near the door is the club's totem animal, an owl, which signifies discretion and wisdom and the cloaked nature of the club's meetings. Over the door is the motto: "Weaving spiders come not here."

Bohemian Club

Lifted from Shakespeare's A *Midsummer Night's Dream*, it warns members to leave business matters at the door before entering.

Dating back to 1872, the Bohemian Club began as a group of newspaper reporters, writers, and artists (bohemians of their day), but soon members realized they needed money to thrive and invited businessmen and elected officials to join. Giannini was a member, and presumably gave the club a loan when its headquarters burned down after the quake. Today the membership list of 2,500 includes George H. W. Bush, Jimmy Buffet, Mark Twain, Jack London, and Walter Cronkite.

The club has earned a controversial reputation for two reasons: 1) Barring women when networking and power brokering clearly take place; 2) The mystery surrounding its annual two-week retreat to the Bohemian Grove, a hidden 2,700-acre tract in the redwoods near the Russian River (about two hours north of the city).

During the retreat, Bohemians enjoy outdoor activities and all kinds of entertainment: plays, variety shows, sing-alongs, etc. There are also lakeside chats on weekends by notables such as Colin Powell, George Schultz, and George W. Bush. Dwight Eisenhower and Richard Nixon gave talks that helped get their presidential campaigns rolling. At night, members bed down at fraternal camps with names such as Mandalay, Silverado Squatters, Ye Merrie Yowls, Hill Billies, Cave Man, Poison Oak, and Lost Angels.

CHAPTER 16.

A MAN, A PLAN, A PALACE, AND AN EXPO: BERNARD MAYBECK

1915

It was a fluke that Bernard Maybeck ended up working on the 1915 Panama–Pacific International Exposition. And in some ways, it wasn't. At 51 he was a highly regarded architect, acclaimed for a host of houses, churches, offices, clubs, and other public buildings, but his idea for the layout of the Panama–Pacific Expo had been rejected. He wasn't selected for the Expo's Architectural Executive Commission either. Instead, his ex-partner and two of his former students (from when he founded the University of California Berkeley's architect and civil engineering school) were chosen. The head of the commission, his longtime friend Willis Polk, offered him a drafter job, which meant he would not get to design any buildings, just draw the blueprints for others' plans. Pressed for income, Maybeck accepted.

It was a move he—and the city's residents and visitors—wouldn't regret.

City merchants and officials cooked up the Panama–Pacific Expo to attract visitors worldwide, make a profit, showcase progress through human invention and hard work, and commemorate the opening of the Panama Canal in 1915. The earthquake in 1906 added a greater purpose: To

Bernard Maybeck

demonstrate to one and all, as President Taft stated after sticking a silver spade in the earth to kickoff the Expo's construction in 1911, that San Francisco was "the city that knows how."

The Expo grounds extended from the Presidio to Fort Mason, the majority an undeveloped area between the two known as Harbor View (today's Marina District). Faced with Harbor View's 625 acres of mudflats and shifting sands, the Expo's architects ordered 300,000 cubic yards of landfill. Golden Gate Park Superintendent John McLaren topped it off with tons of topsoil, 30,000 trees, and imported plants such as Canary Island Date Palms that joined California Fan Palms in doubles rows to create the half-mile-long Avenue of the Palms.

Since all of the Expo's structures were to be temporary, the architects selected inexpensive building materials: wood, sand, and an imitation travertine composed of hemp plaster and gypsum. They also picked an architectural style: Beaux Arts.

Described as an "idyllic city on a fill" by one pundit, the Expo was divided into four sections: foreign and state pavilions, athletic fields and livestock paddocks, a "Joy Zone," made up of amusements and concessions, and 11 great exhibit halls labeled palaces.

Polk was assigned to design the Palace of Fine Arts, which would greet people and set the tone for the Expo. Perhaps he was too overworked as head of the architectural commission or perhaps he was just plain stumped. For whatever reason, Polk threw the design open to the drafters in his office, requesting sketches from all who wanted the assignment. Maybeck entered the competition.

How do you design a temporary building that reflects the past and future yet is timeless? Maybeck believed it needed an emotional character, "that of sadness modified by the feeling that beauty has a soothing influence."

And so, with San Francisco re-creating itself out of its earthquake ruins, he drafted "a Greek temple in the middle of a small mountain lake" that would evoke "an old Roman ruin, away from civilization."

The office reviewed all the submissions, then voted. It was unanimous: Maybeck's charcoal sketch was superior. He was elected architect of the Palace of Fine Arts.

Maybeck designed a domed edifice ringed with a lagoon as "the crux of the whole composition." He landscaped his creation with trees and ice plant, intending that "the foliage should be high and romantic, avoiding all stiff lines." And he placed 18-foot-tall sculptures of weeping women around planter boxes atop the palace's colonnades to underscore his theme of melancholy. Guards were instructed to tell visitors that the maidens were "crying over the sadness of art."

The interior of the building's 135-foot-high rotunda contained eight murals. Four illustrated the conception and birth of art through symbolic groups of figures and alternated with murals of California's four "golds": metal nuggets, poppies, citrus fruits, and wheat. The hues of the complex adhered to the official eight-color palette set by the architectural commission including: terra cotta for domes, dark cerulean blue for ceiling vaults and recessed panels, brown-speckled light red for the background of colonnades, and gold for statues.

On January 15, 1915, the Panama Canal opened. A few weeks later, at 6 a.m. on February 20, Mayor "Sunny Jim" Rolph led a legion of marching bands and 150,000 people up

Rotunda, altar, and colonnade of the Palace of Fine Arts, 1915

Panama Pacific International Exposition Opening Day, 1915

Van Ness Avenue to the Expo gate. At high noon, from Washington, DC, President Woodrow Wilson tapped a gold telegraph key to turn on the fair's lights and machinery. The gates were released and the Panama–Pacific Expo commenced—on schedule and under budget. By the end of the day, 250,000 people (more than half the city's population) had tromped the grounds. More than 18 million people followed during the Expo's ten-month run, placing it solidly in the black.

For their 50 cents (25 cents for children), visitors could venture wherever their fancy took them. They could view gardens and displays about science, industry, art, and world cultures. They could experience new-fangled devices by taking a plane or submarine ride or making a transcontinental phone call. They could enter the Court of the Universe through the Arch of the Rising Sun (signifying the achievements of the "Oriental peoples") or by Arch of the Setting Sun (signifying the achievements of the "Western nations"). If they wandered into the Palace of Machinery, they could watch a Model T Ford being assembled every ten minutes. In the Palace of Liberal Arts at the Underwood Exhibit, they witnessed news stories being typed on a 14-ton typewriter—1,728 times larger than normal.

Day or night, fairgoers could hit the Joy Zone, where the hot tickets were an educational Panama Canal Ride, replete with headphones playing an audio track from a phonograph and the Aeroscope, which employed a giant steel arm to hoist a car of passengers two stories high to view the cityscape. At the 4,000-seat Festival Hall, they could listen to conductor John Philip Sousa.

When night descended, interior and exterior lighting infused new romanticism to the scene. General Electric lighting designer Walter D'Arcy Ryan's "Scintillator" projected 48 multi-colored rays of light onto the Expo's buildings. Composed of a bevy of floodlights with color filters and housed on a barge, the Scintillator beamed a different color to each exhibit hall's courtyard through fog. If San Francisco's habitual fog didn't materialize, a steam train provided it. The Scintillator also spotlighted the belle of the ball, the Tower of Jewels. A lofty 435 feet and studded with 102,000 glittering "Novagems"—multi-colored Austrian cut-glass prisms mounted to move freely with the breeze—the tower refracted sunlight by day and reflected the Scintillator's rays by night.

The Tower of Jewels awed visitors, but the most popular Expo building was Maybeck's Palace of Fine Arts. "It is the vision of a painter who is also a poet, worked out in terms of architecture," one Expo designer explained. Thomas Edison put it more directly, "The architect of that building is a genius. There is not the equal of it anywhere on earth."

Arial view of the main group of exhibition palaces of the Panama Pacific International Exposition, c. 1914

Tower of Jewels, 1915

Maybeck's palace was so popular that before "Taps" was trumpeted from the Tower of Jewels at midnight to close out the Expo on December 4, 1915, philanthropist Phoebe Hearst formed the Palace Preservation League to preserve it. The business community, counting on real estate profits in the new landfilled area, worked to have the Palace demolished as planned along with the rest of the Expo's buildings. Owing to the Preservation League, the public's will, and its placement on U.S. Army land, the Palace of Fine Arts was saved. Because it was designed to be temporary, it has had to be saved a few more times—including a total reconstruction in 1964 and a seismic retrofit in 2009.

Maybeck's palace is one part of his legacy, as are the works of his students, who carried on his beliefs in what is now termed sustainable design. As writer-lecturer-architect Sarah Susanka put it, "Beauty is the most sustainable act you can perform, because when something is beautiful, people will look after it. Because of ... the beauty of his designs, we'll be looking after his legacy for generations to come."

JULIA MORGAN

The most outstanding of Maybeck's Cal Berkeley students was Julia Morgan. In 1894, when she earned her degree in civil engineering, she was the only woman in her class. Maybeck encouraged her to follow in his footsteps and go to the elite L'Ecole des Beaux-Arts in Paris. She did and was its first female graduate. Morgan opened an office in the Merchants Exchange Building downtown (its ballroom is named after her) and designed many buildings in San Francisco after the 'quake (including redesigning the Fairmont Hotel) and around the Bay Area for many years following. Her most famous creation is La Cuesta Encantada in San Simeon, better known as Hearst Castle. Indefatigable, she designed nearly 750 buildings—almost quadruple the total of her mentor Maybeck.

CHAPTER 17.

BECOMING INA COOLBRITH: CALIFORNIA'S FIRST POET LAUREATE

1841–1928

On June 29, 1915, an elderly woman in a black dress with a sash embroidered with bright orange California poppies—the emblem of the Women's Press Association— laid her black plumed hat on her chair and was escorted to a stage of San Francisco's Panama-Pacific International Expo. The president of the University of California made a short speech about the old woman to an audience of the Congress of Authors and Journalists, finishing with "therefore upon thee so worthy do I confer this laurel crown and name thee Poet Laureate of California." The packed crowd cheered, wept, and waved white handkerchiefs. And so, Ina Coolbrith, at 74, became the first poet laureate in the history of the United States.

The audience that day knew all about Coolbrith's volumes of poems, her unflagging support of fellow writers, her literary salon, and her editing of literary journals. What they didn't know was the path she traveled to arrive in her beloved city of "mists and of dreams." The facts of Coolbrith's birth and childhood only came to light after her death on Leap Day in 1928.

Coolbrith's mother, Agnes Moulton Coolbrith, grew up in rural Maine and

Clockwise from top left: Ina Coolbrith c. 1870, Joaquin Miller, Gertrude Atherton, Jack London, Isadora Duncan, Mark Twain

took off for Boston as a young woman where she encountered a new religion—the Church of the Latter Day Saints—illuminated by a pair of young, male missionaries. Agnes converted and headed to Kirtland, Ohio, with other Mormons, to create a new Zion. She married Don Carlos Smith, brother of Joseph Smith, Jr., founder of the LDS Church, and had two daughters.

Vigilante gangs, unchecked by the state, attacked the Zionists. The Smiths and other Mormons fled to Far West, Missouri to erect another new Zion. The violent acts continued and they escaped to Nauvoo, Illinois, to construct yet another new Zion. Here, on March 10, 1841, Josephine Donna Smith was born. Known by her pet name "Ina," Coolbrith (a name she took later), lost her father to pneumonia four months later.

As Mormon tradition required, Agnes married her husband's brother, becoming Joseph Smith's seventh wife. In 1844 a mob murdered him in his jail cell and gangs began to terrorize the Zionists once again. In a poem years later, Coolbrith summarized the period as a "sorrow and song of frightening childhood."

While Brigham Young, the new Mormon leader, prepared his flock to resettle in the far west, Agnes left the LDS church to marry William Pickett, a non-Mormon. He made her vow never to mention her Mormon past. To protect her family, Coolbrith kept silent about her early childhood the rest of her life.

She also never revealed the exciting tale of how she arrived in California.

From left: A young Coolbrith; the Expulsion of Mormons from Nauvoo, Illinois

In 1851, Coolbrith's stepfather caught Gold Fever and the family lumbered west for seven months in a covered wagon. In Nevada they met African-American scout Jim Beckwourth, who had just created a new shortcut through the Sierra Nevada mountains. Coolbrith's family was the first party he led through. At the crest of the pass, Beckwourth put Coolbrith in front of him on his horse and pointed, "There, little girl, there is California! There is your kingdom." They rode down the mountain and she became the first child of settlers to enter the state.

The family lived in Marysville near Ina Mine, her father's gold claim, then in San Francisco where a thief burnt down their house, prompting their relocation to Los Angeles. Here Ina—growing into a beauty—opened a ball for Pio Pico, California's last Mexican governor. Two years later she forged a disastrous marriage to Robert Carsely, an ironworker and actor. Their infant son died. Carsely accused her (falsely) of infidelity and tried to kill her with a knife and then a gun, culminating in her stepfather shooting Carsely in the hand. A much publicized divorce trial annulled the marriage in 1861 and in 1862, the family decamped to San Francisco.

Coolbrith taught English at a primary school and crafted a few poems that the *California Home Journal* published. She never spoke of her marriage or her son. Instead, she changed her name to Ina Donna Coolbrith and began the life that made her famous.

Coolbrith attended Unitarian services preached by Thomas Starr King, a fervent abolitionist who died at 40 for his efforts. She wrote a poem memorializing him and at his funeral befriended two other writers who did the same: Bret Harte who deemed her "the sweetest note in California literature" and Charles Warren Stoddard. Dubbed "The Golden Gate Trinity" the trio became a magnetic nucleus that attracted luminaries such as Mark Twain, John Muir, and Lotta Crabtree.

Coolbrith helped Harte edit the literary magazine *The Overland Monthly* and took the then little-known poet Joaquin Miller under her wing. In 1865, in her family's Russian Hill home, Coolbrith started a literary circle to draw together new writers and introduce them to publishers declaring, "I want the Circle to live and be ever widening ... to perpetually keep the history and literature ... of California alive..."

In 1873, she put out her first volume of poetry, *A Perfect Day, and Other Poems*. Then, after a scant ten years in the literary world, the death of her widowed sister in January 1874 curtailed her creative output for decades. Coolbrith stepped up to support her mother and her sister's two children. Her poems brought $20 apiece, not enough to sustain her family. Coolbrith had a wry attitude about it all as a short piece printed in the *San Francisco Star* attests:

Fan: "Oh Miss Coolbrith, our family just lives on your poems!"

"How nice," she smiled, "that is more than I was ever able to do."

Later in 1874, the Board of Directors of the Oakland Library proffered a position as the city's first librarian. Coolbrith accepted the $80-a-month job (around $1,600 today), and moved her family to the "Athens of the Pacific," as Oakland was then referred to.

It was a demanding six days-a-week job in a library building that housed a chess room and a ladies' parlor along with the usual reading room. Coolbrith encouraged countless readers, particularly the young, to follow their interests and enjoy where books took them. She influenced Isadora Duncan whose father was smitten with her (as were many other men, but Coolbrith remained unmarried). She also encouraged Jack London, who later recalled, "Nobody at home bothered their heads over what I read ... one day at the library I drew out a volume on Pizarro in Peru ... as you handed it to me you praised me for reading books of that nature ... If you only knew how proud your words made me! You were a goddess to me."

In 1892, a new Board of Directors rewarded Coolbrith for her 18 years of service with a three-day notice to quit the premises. Although one director groused, "We need a librarian, not a poet," Ina's real crime was giving an off-the-cuff interview to a reporter about the dilapidated library's need for repairs. The dismissal strained her finances for years. She gleaned part time librarian work, was guest of honor at events across the U.S., and survived a life-threatening bout of pneumonia. Between 1894 and 1895 she brought out two new volumes of poetry: *The Singer of the Sea* and *Songs from the Golden Gate*.

In 1899, Coolbrith obtained work from the male-only Bohemian Club, who had made her an honorary member 25 years earlier out of respect for her poetry (she composed "Bohemia" about them) and the curtains she sewed for them, and she returned to San Francisco..

By 1906, she was settled back on her beloved Russian Hill with her female caretaker and finishing a semi-autobiographical history of California literature when the big quake struck. They escaped with their cats and a few belongings but the fire destroyed the house. Coolbrith never rewrote the history book remarking, "Were I to write what I know, the book would be too sensational to print, but were I to write what I think proper, it would be too dull to read."

Ina Coolbrith, 1880s

Well-to-do novelist Gertrude Atherton and Coolbrith's Bohemian Club allies built her a new house on Russian Hill, where, in 1909, she resumed penning poetry and holding the Ina Coolbrith Circle while others set her poems to music.

She was elected president of the Pacific Coast Women's Press Association in 1911 and president of the Congress of Authors and Journalists in 1915. In 1919, the state legislature officially decreed Coolbrith the "Loved, Laurel-Crowned Poet of California."

She continued to pour herself into her poetry and mentor young writers until her death in 1928. In 1932, the U.S. Geographic Board name designated an 8,000-foot peak near Beckwourth Pass as Mount Ina Coolbrith. The Ina Coolbrith Circle continues to this day, UC Santa Cruz hands out an annual Ina Coolbrith Memorial Poetry Prize, and a secluded park with a view high on Russian Hill is named Ina Coolbrith Park. But the final words should go to Coolbrith, from her last volume of poems, *Wings of Sunset*, published posthumously in 1929.

What use the questioning? this thing we are:
  A breath called life, housed for a little space
In how infinitesimal a star;
    Then vanished, leaving neither sound nor trace.

CHAPTER 18.

DON'T CALL IT THE ROCK: THE ALCATRAZ KIDS

1934–1963

"All of us are glad to get off. Alcatraz was never no good for nobody."
–Frank Weatherman, last prisoner to exit the island when the prison closed on March 21, 1963

"It was a great place to grow up...There were parties for the kids, formal dances for the teens. We were within steps of the prison but no one locked their doors."
–Pat Bergen-Rothschild, a child on the island from 1939–1952

As Spanish explorer Juan Manuel de Ayala sailed around the San Francisco Bay in 1775, he surveyed what he saw, naming the 22-acre island one and a half miles off the mainland La Isla de los Alcatraces, (the Island of the Pelicans). The area's Ohlone and Miwok Indians considered the island taboo, believing it was cursed, and stayed away. For centuries the pelicans, gulls, and herons had the run of the place, until 1850, when the U.S. Army claimed it for the next eighty-three years. The Army built a citadel, which included a fort and a prison. The fort saw little action but the prison housed

Civil War soldiers and a mounted Rodman gun at Fort of Alcatraz, and Alcatraz Island, 1895

a variety of inmates over the years: deserting soldiers, Native Americans, Confederate sympathizers and prisoners during the Civil War, military prisoners and convalescents from the war in the Philippines at the turn of the century, and conscientious objectors during WWI.

By 1933 and in the grip of the Depression, the War Department concluded that the place was too costly and offloaded the island to the Department of Justice for free. J. Edgar Hoover was ecstatic: Alcatraz would be the perfect home for public enemies like Al Capone, Arthur "Doc" Barker, and George "Machine Gun" Kelly, who were too out of control for federal penitentiaries such as Leavenworth and Lewisburg.

On August 22, 1934, Warden James A. Johnston and thirty guards, along with federal marshals and sixty special FBI agents, ushered the first bunch of prisoners into the re-furbished prison. But the guards, inmates, and warden weren't alone on the island. Alcatraz was also home to fifty-two families, including 126 women and children whose fathers were guards or assistant wardens. Most families lived in one of three large apartment buildings, which offered sixty furnished apartments at $25 a month with free utilities.

"At the time, these kids did not really think there was anything unusual or special about where they were growing up," Scott Cornfield, who lived on the island as a child, stated in an interview about *Children of Alcatraz*, the documentary he made in 2003. The grown children, then in their 50s

Public enemies at Alcatraz (from left): Al Capone, Arthur "Doc" Barker, and George "Machine Gun" Kelly

through 70s, he interviewed in his film were solidly positive about the experience. They likened living on Alcatraz to a small town community where everyone was family and no one locked their doors. They resented the way it was portrayed in the movies as Hellcatraz and Uncle Sam's Devil's Island and never would call it "The Rock."

Just like other kids, when they weren't doing homework, the kids on Alcatraz played games: baseball, football, basketball. One game they played that was different: Prison. Taking the part of a guard was preferable to being the convict.

They had two playgrounds; the bigger one had been the Army's parade ground. Both were made of concrete, so they roller skated a lot. At times they would roll though hairpins turns from the cement yard below the warden's house all the way down to the bottom of the hill. Toy guns were forbidden—holsters were okay—so they improvised with bananas, fingers, and popsicle sticks. They also sang songs about the island:

"On the isle of Alcatraz I met him,
Beneath the shade of the old prison wall.
I can still see the guards hanging 'round him
T'was goodbye to the con I adored."

After 5:30, when the prison went into lockdown, children and adults could go over to the Social Hall (Officers' Club). On the first floor there were two

Correctional officers' children on a cannon at the south end of the Island, c. 1940s-50s

pool tables, a ping-pong table, a two-lane bowling alley, and a snack bar. The second floor had a movie theatre (the prisoners watched the film during the day) as well as a dining hall and dance floor. There were plays, a bowling league, "Happy Rock Kids" (a children's theatre group), spring dances, watermelon feasts, holiday and birthday celebrations, and weddings.

With the strict rules and the threat of being hauled before the warden if they broke them, the parents believed their children were safer on the fenced island than on the mainland and couldn't get into any trouble. However like all kids, those on Alcatraz found ways to break the rules. They ventured to forbidden places all over the island—onto the cliffs, into coves, and down to the beach. They clambered over transoms to get into the prisoners' store room, crept above the apartments in the crawl space, and snuck into the Social Hall to play "Spin the Bottle." They told their schoolmates in San Francisco that a secret tunnel ran from Van Ness Avenue to the island.

"You think you are just ordinary," explained Cornfield, "until all of a sudden, all the kids in school want to come to your house." The Alcatraz kids commuted to schools in San Francisco by boats that made twelve daily trips to the Van Ness Street Pier. (Their parents used them too, to shop for food and goods not available at the small island store.) The kids could invite friends over but they had to be checked on and off by a roster. Since Alcatraz was typically colder, wetter, and foggier than the city, occasionally the boats didn't run. The kids loved this as it meant no school.

The children came into contact with the prisoners daily as they worked around the island—even getting to know them by name. These were the "trustees," the well-behaved convicts assigned garbage detail and other jobs at the warden and residents' homes. The kids weren't supposed to interact with the inmates, but at times their lives intersected. Some prisoners rescued balls for them or gave them small presents in the form of bric-a-brac they found in their work or flowers.

When Al Capone arrived, chained and shackled, on railroad car towed on a barge from Oakland in 1934, the kids couldn't believe the high security. Still, they spotted the short, fat gangster as he boarded Black Marie, the inmates' bus to the prison at the top of the hill.

From time to time, raucous songs, screams, and other noises emanated from the prison. When the children asked about the racket, their fathers simply told them not to worry. If a siren went off, everyone knew there was an escape in progress. When the kids woke up, their mothers would tell them, "Go back to sleep. Your dad will be home in a while."

Inmates passing through metal detectors on the way from the prison yard to the industry buildings., c. 1935-1960.

In May 1946, six prisoners botched a breakout and took two guards hostage, igniting a two-day riot dubbed "The Battle of Alcatraz." Hundreds of

Alcatraz Island

guards were re-enforced by twenty-eight sharpshooters, eighty Marines, five Coast Guard ships, two Navy destroyers, and city police. Most kids were in school and frightened about their fathers. Two children were on the island and saw their fathers shot. In the end, three prisoners and two guards were killed and one prisoner was injured along with seventeen guards.

Afterwards, rules tightened, which was tough on the kids. They were scared of the inmates and observed the "no contact" rule. Ernie Lageson recalls one "big, heavy, strong Nordic" prisoner in Cornfield's film: "After the riot the kids would not talk to him and were afraid of him. He actually lost his mind over it and had to be transferred to the mental facility in Springfield. As he was taken away [he said] 'my little friends won't talk to me anymore.'"

But life on Alcatraz wasn't always focused on the prison. The children witnessed the dredging of Treasure Island and the construction of the Bay Bridge, and of course the Golden Gate Bridge, which they skated over once it opened. They saw the *China Clipper* (a flying mail boat) thunder across the bay and Amelia Earhart take off. They observed the fleet leaving and returning for WWII.

Every year many of the children who grew up on the island meet up as part of the Alcatraz Alumni Association's annual August reunion. A few guards and inmates show up too, and they all reminisce, animosities long-obliterated by their shared past. "You were living in the middle of San Francisco Bay," remarks Jolene Babyak, who grew up on the island in the '50s and '60s and returns for the reunions. "Even today I can come out of the cell house on a perfectly clear night and it literally takes your breath away ... we had an absolutely criminal view."

CHAPTER 19.

SHAPE UP, SHIP OUT, AND STRIKE: HARRY BRIDGES

1934

"I was just a working stiff who happened to be around at the right time."
                    –Harry Bridges, Labor organizer and negotiator

July 5, 1934, became known as "Bloody Thursday" after police fired into a throng of 5,000 dock workers on strike at the Embarcadero. This sorry day in San Francisco would change labor rights forever, thanks, in large part, to the efforts of Harry Bridges.

Born in Melbourne, Australia, in 1901, as a teenager Bridges assisted his father in collecting rents from poor tenants, a task he abhorred. Instead, he was keen on socialism and Jack London tales. At 16, he split for the sea. As a merchant seaman roaming the seaports of the world, he witnessed poverty firsthand. "The more I saw, the more I knew that there was something wrong with the system," he concluded.

In the early '20s, Bridges settled down in San Francisco and worked as stevedore at the wharf. He got married, started a family, and endured an unsuccessful strike by his union. The hiring system was stacked against

Harry Bridges

"casuals" (freelancers) like Bridges who comprised 75 percent of the available workforce. At daybreak every morning, jobseekers flocked to the dock gates for the heavily resented "shape up." Gang bosses ambled out to select the day's hires, favoring those in the Star Gangs—the other 25 percent of the workforce—who provided them liquor, kickbacks, and other favors, and who were members of the Waterfront Employers Association.

If hired, stevedores often experienced the "speed-up," a killer pace maintained by the Walking Boss, who frequently pitted crews against each other to see who could load faster. If workers complained, couldn't keep up, got injured, or were believed to support a workers' union, they were written up in the Blue Book, a work history the company maintained on each worker. Companies hired longshoremen with "clean books" only.

Shipping and stevedoring companies bragged that San Francisco had the most cost-efficient longshoremen in the U.S., crowing that 100-men crews routinely loaded 3,000-ton steamships in two days and a night and sixteen-men gangs moved more than 20 tons an hour by hand. Throughout the 1920s, three to six longshoremen were disabled for every eight hours on the job. Most workers didn't report accidents for fear of being blacklisted. Still, annually, the number of reported accidents equaled the number of workers. Bridges joined the ILA (International Longshoremen's Association) in 1922—a small, deflated union since losing a strike in 1919—and was blacklisted after marching under its banner in the 1924 Labor Day parade. To keep his family afloat, Bridges joined the company union in 1927 and worked as a winch operator and rigger on a steel-handling gang. As the Depression descended and President Franklin Roosevelt's National Industrial Recovery Act, which forbade employers from penalizing employees for unionizing, passed in 1933, the ILA revived itself. Thousands joined the newly chartered San Francisco local—95 percent of the city's longshoremen.

Bridges got elected to the board of executives and began organizing an alliance of maritime unions up and down the Pacific ports. "All workers must stand together," he preached.

"There can be no discrimination because of race, color, creed, national origin, religious or political belief. Discrimination is the weapon of the boss."

By 1934, as a result of the Depression, 50 percent of longshoremen were either unemployed or eking out a living on a $10-a-week pay. In February, Bridges spoke at the convention San Francisco hosted for maritime employees and helped craft the resulting set of demands for the employers: $1 per hour wage, 6-hour day, a 30-hour workweek, a coast-wide contract, and that all hiring be conducted through a union hall (which would effectively end the shape up). As negotiations began, Bridges, his board, and rank-and-file union members prepared for a strike. And the shipping companies prepared to squelch it and stamp out labor organizing for good.

On May 9, 1934, with negotiations going nowhere, an estimated 12,000 dockworkers from San Diego to Seattle went on strike. Three days later, the

Picket parade on the Embarcadero, May 10, 1934

Howard S. Sperry and Nickolas Bordoise were killed during a waterfront workers strike on July 5, 1934, on what became known as "Bloody Thursday."

seaman joined them, and the Teamsters Union refused to drive their trucks across their picket lines. It was the first industry-wide strike in history.

By mid-May, 35,000 workers were out, the ports were paralyzed, and Bridges, as chair of the Joint Marine Strike Committee, was in charge. The companies, backed by city, state, and federal officials, retaliated by embedding strikebreakers on ships, infiltrating the union, using Red-baiting and other intimidation tactics, and setting hundreds of police and thugs on the picketers. As negotiations stalled, clashes between armed police and picketers escalated. Perishable goods rotted, as strikebreakers couldn't work amidst the congestion of picketers, police, and thousands of tons of goods piling up at the docks.

The work stoppage was costing the city $700,000 each day (around $170 million today). Banker William H. Crocker believed that it was the best thing that ever happened to San Francisco. "It's costing us money, certainly. But it's a good investment, a marvelous investment," he said. "It's solving the labor problem for years to come, perhaps forever. When the men have been driven back to their jobs, we won't have to worry about them anymore.

They'll have learned their lesson. Labor in San Francisco is licked."

It was time to push back the union, Mayor Angelo Rossi decided. On July 3, he ordered the Industrial Association, the arm of the maritime corporations responsible for crushing the 1919 ILA strike, to open the port. On Thursday morning, July 5, the association filled trucks with strikebreakers and rolled onto the Embarcadero, determined to get goods moving again. With the aid of the police, who lobbed tear gas bombs and sprayed a vomit-inducing gas, the strikebreakers managed to get some cargo on to the trucks and railroad cars and over to warehouses.

Strikers fought back by burning trucks and dumping cargo. Police began clubbing people, and strikers threw up barricades and hurled bricks, cobblestones, and railroad spikes. By the afternoon the battle hit its peak when police drew their shotguns and pistols. Firing into the crowd of 5,000 picketers, they injured hundreds and killed two men—a stevedore and an unemployed cook who had been volunteering at the ILA strike kitchen.

The day became known as "Bloody Thursday."

The next Monday, an honor guard of WWI veterans led a funeral procession for the two slain men of some 30,000 marchers who walked in silence to Beethoven's "Funeral March." "In life they wouldn't have commanded a second glance on the streets of San Francisco," a reporter wrote of the two slain workers, "but in death they were borne the length of Market Street in a stupendous and reverential procession that astounded the city."

With public opinion shifted, the employers offered to arbitrate with the ILA. Unwilling to ditch the seamen and teamsters who had stood by their side, the union, led by Bridges, called for arbitration to include all maritime unions. The employers turned this down and the state governor ordered 4,600 National Guard troops equipped with "whippets" (small tanks) mounted with machine guns, to the city. The ILA, along with 116 other San Francisco unions, voted for a "General Strike," which began on July 16. For three days San Francisco (along with Alameda County, which includes the cities of Berkeley and Oakland) was shutdown. Workers across the city walked off their jobs—butchers, boilermakers, cooks, shop workers, secretaries, and 2,600 laundry workers. Signs in the windows of mom-and-

Harry Bridges leads Labor Day Parade on Market Street in 1939

pop stores all around the city read "No business until the boys win!" and "Closed for the duration."

The ports remained at a standstill, as did streetcars, taxis and all public transportation. Strikers blocked all highways, allowing only emergency vehicles in. Theaters, liquor stores and all but 19 of the city's 200 restaurants shut their doors. Governor Merriam telegrammed President Franklin Roosevelt: "Bolshevik army has invaded San Francisco. Federal troops needed. Urgent." Roosevelt reportedly told his secretary, "Wire the good governor not to excite himself. There is no invading army. That's just Harry Bridges."

Having demonstrated its strength, the unions' Labor Council called off the General Strike after three days. Two days later, the companies agreed to arbitrate with all the longshoreman unions. Since the offer excluded seamen, Bridges objected, but was overridden by the ILA membership's overwhelming vote for arbitration. On July 29, as agreements began to be hammered out, San Francisco's waterfront workers returned to work. Within days, other port cities saw their workers back on the job.

On October 12, the Longshoreman's Board announced the results of the arbitration. Wages went up, hours went down, and the Blue Book and shape up were history, replaced with a joint employer-union hiring hall. Bridges, who regularly admonished others to "Put your faith in the rank and file," began a long career as a well-respected and incorruptible union leader.

Today, Longshore workers' unions continue to observe Bloody Thursday by not working. Container shipping has moved the majority of the port work to Oakland. On July 28, 2001, (what would have been Bridges' 100th birthday) Governor Gray Davis decreed Harry Bridges Day, and the mayor of San Francisco dedicated Harry Bridges Plaza at the Embarcadero. Close by, at

Steuart and Mission, is Injury to One, a commemorative sculpture with a plaque inscribed, "In memory of Howard Sperry and Nick Bordoise, who gave their lives on Bloody Thursday, July 5, 1934, so that all working people might enjoy a greater measure of dignity and security."

CHAPTER 20.

PAINTING THE TOWN'S BRIDGE RED: JOSEPH STRAUSS

1937

"When you build a bridge, you build something for all time."

–Joseph Strauss

Joseph Strauss' mother was a pianist, his father a painter and writer. Like his Bavarian Buckeye parents, Strauss wanted to be an artist, so he wrote poetry. Later, while studying economics at the University of Cincinnati, he wanted to play football. But with his slender, 5-foot 3-inch frame, he landed in the infirmary. While convalescing, he became riveted watching the construction of the Cincinnati-Covington Bridge, the nation's first long-span suspension bridge. Strauss had discovered his true artistic calling.

After college and a few drafting jobs, Strauss became an expert engineer of the bascule, or seesaw, type of drawbridge. Substituting cement for iron for the counterweights, he revolutionized its design. He founded his own firm and built drawbridges over rivers from the Cuyahoga in Ohio to the Neva in Russia—400 in total. But his biggest creation—and biggest challenge—was yet to come.

Aerial view of the Golden Gate, the Presidio of San Francisco, and the city of San Francisco, 1915

With more than a half million people in 1925, San Francisco needed to connect to the opposite banks of its great bay in order to grow like Los Angeles, its quickly expanding competitor. It was the age of the auto, with a Model T rolling off the assembly line every 10 seconds. Cars and people clogged the bay's ferries, which weren't able to keep up, even with 50 million crossings a year. Committees in the East Bay cities of Oakland and Berkeley were clamoring for a bridge, as were those in the Redwood Empire towns north of the Golden Gate.

Strauss jumped at the chance to design a bridge for the Golden Gate. He submitted drawings, along with a low bid that the San Francisco Board of Supervisors rejected. His design, a variation on a bascule bridge, resembled "an upside-down rat trap" in one reviewer's eyes. Registering his commitment, however, the supervisors told him to proceed, as long as he accepted input from other engineers and raised money.

Strauss went to bat for the Golden Gate Bridge, tirelessly promoting it at meetings and in media all around the bay. "A great city with water barriers and no bridges is like a skyscraper with no elevators," he argued in a radio address. "Bridges are a monument to progress."

But Strauss faced a headwind of skepticism from many directions. Fellow engineers believed the Golden Gate's channel was too deep, its current too strong, and a one-mile suspension bridge too long. The War Department was sure the bridge would crumple and obstruct the bay. Public opposition took the form of isolation and exceptionality. "In the interest of your own uniqueness, dear San Franciscans," writer Katherine Gerould implored, "do not bridge the Golden Gate." The supervisors weren't convinced, so Strauss hired a fixer who overcame reluctance with bribes.

In 1929, the city signed Strauss as the chief engineer of the Golden Gate Bridge project. The next year, despite the Depression, the Redwood Empire counties voted for a $35-million-dollar bond (around $488 million today) to cover its construction. A.P. Giannini's Bank of America backed the bond and the Redwood Empire counties put up property as security.

The ace team of architects, geologists, and engineers that Strauss hired went to work confronting the bridge's challenges. Strong ocean currents and winds that whipped at up to 100 miles per hour posed significant problems. Leon Moissieff, a renowned suspension bridge engineer from New York, performed the force calculations necessary to solve the wind stress problems. Devising the bridge's cables, suspender ropes, towers, and abutments to be counterweighted by the suspended roadbed, Moissieff drafted a narrow, sleek bridge that was light and flexible enough to contend with any gale.

Professor Charles Ellis, a structural engineer and mathematician from Chicago, turned Moissieff's visionary drawings into a practical plan. Working with a slide rule and a hand-cranked adding machine, Ellis performed the calculations to draw the blueprints. He stressed about every technical aspect, testing as much as possible to allay his fears. When he was done and still obsessing, Strauss banished him to Chicago, where Ellis

Joseph Strauss (second from right), with A.H. Ammann, Charles Derleth, Jr., Leon F. Moiseiff, and Andrew C. Lawson

continued to finesse the specifications even after Strauss fired him.

Residential architect Irving Morrow was the third important member of Strauss's team. Morrow shaped the bridge's towers and infused an Art Deco scheme into the lighting, railings, and walkways. Most important, arguably, he wrestled Strauss to the mat on the paint color. Silver or gray were standard choices. For maximum visibility for ships, the Navy wanted yellow with black stripes. Strauss, accustomed to the grime of Chicago, where he'd worked on most of his bridges, insisted on black to hide the dirt. Exposing metal panels to the salty climate, Morrow performed numerous paint tests and proposed what he termed "international orange"—the red color we're familiar with today.

Construction began on January 5, 1933, with Strauss overseeing the day-to-day progress. Aware of the hazardous conditions—wind, fog, and cold that combined to make the iron as slippery as ice—he pioneered the use of safety devices: safety belts, lines, and nets, glare-free goggles, hard hats, and a protective hand lotion. Anyone who didn't use the gear was terminated.

The first order of business was to excavate 3,250,000 cubic feet of dirt and set the anchorages to pin down the ends of the bridge. Aided by the "elephant trunk," a long metal tube that spouted wet cement, workers smoothed the 90,000 cubic feet of concrete to form each 12-story anchorage.

In November, the north tower—anchored to the Marin County headlands—began to rise. Working from a trestle, divers set bombs to blast rock out of the sea and build the concrete piling needed for the south (San Francisco) tower. Once erected, the 745-foot towers stood astride the channel like spires reaching for the sky. Once each tower fit its base, a gang of riveters hammered 600,000 rivets to secure it. Every four-person rivet gang was bossed by a "heater" who warmed the rivets on a forge and tossed them into a "catcher's" tin can. "They went "Zing!" just like a bullet ... scare hell out of you when that rivet is coming," ironworker Walter Vestnys recalled. "And you best catch it, and take it out, and ... put it in fast."

In June 1935, with both towers riveted in, it was time to spin the 80,000 miles of wire—about the width of a pencil—spooled at the bridge site into the two 36-inch main cables that would span the bridge. To accomplish this, a spinning wheel plucked a loop of wire out of the spool, lofted it across

Construction of the Golden Gate Bridge: Cable spinning, and men in uniforms pointing to the unfinished Golden Gate Bridge, Fort Scott, c. 1930s

the tops of the two towers and then descended with it to the anchorage. Precision was paramount in order to transfer the bridge's weight to the anchorages according to Ellis's specifications. When the last wire was spun over the span, workers festooned the spinning wheel with flags.

While all this was going on, Strauss vanished for six months. The bridge's directors lamented his whereabouts in the papers and onsite engineers and inspectors oversaw construction. The dozen years of promoting the bridge, overseeing its design, and keeping it financially afloat had taken a toll on Strauss. Finally, he wired from New York and returned, sporadically.

May 27, 1937, kicked off a weeklong fiesta for the bridge's opening. Called "Pedestrians' Day" or "Preview Day," it saw 200,000 people traverse the bridge by foot (backwards and forwards), roller skates, unicycle, and stilts. The next day, Strauss formally presented the bridge to its new owner, the Highway District. At noon, President Franklin D. Roosevelt pressed a telegraph key to signal the start of automobile traffic. Cars crossed the bridge from the north and the south, planes soared over it, and ships breezed under it, all exalting in its debut. Strauss wrote a commemorative poem titled "The Mighty Task is Done."

Opening Day on the Golden Gate Bridge: May 27, 1937

Less than a year later he was dead, having taken full credit for the bridge. Moissieff died four years later, destroyed by the twisting collapse of his Tacoma Narrows Bridge in Puget Sound. Ignored in the festivities and unacknowledged for his contribution, Ellis never saw the bridge and was finally given credit as the lead designer in 2007. The eminent California historian Kevin Starr sums up the triumph of the bridge most clearly:

"The Golden Gate Bridge means many things. It means the victory of San Francisco over its environment. It means San Francisco remains competitive. It means that people can cross the channel more easily. But it also means something else. It celebrates in a mysterious way man's creativity and the joy and wonder of being on this planet."

HALFWAY-TO-HELL CLUB

When a worker fell to his death from a bridge, workers said "He has gone to hell." Strauss designed a cantilevered safety net to catch anyone who fell. In the first few weeks of building the "bed"–the roadway portion of the bridge–ten men plunged into the net. Six were okay, four required hospitalization. At St. Luke's Hospital,

jubilant over their survival, they created the Halfway-to-Hell Club. By the end of construction, the club had nineteen members. The nets buoyed morale and left the record with one death (before they were put up), until a few months before the end of construction, when a large piece of heavy metal staging sheared off, pulling a dozen men and the safety net into the ocean. Two men survived to join the club.

CHAPTER 21.

TEA AND NO SYMPATHY: THE HAGIWARAS AND THEIR GARDEN

1941–1945

On December 7, 1941, Joltin' Joe DiMaggio from North Beach was sitting pretty after his fifty-six-game hitting streak and winning his sixth All-Star award in six years with the New York Yankees. George Hagiwara was serving tea at the Japanese Tea Garden in Golden Gate Park, as his family had done since 1895. Fleishhacker Pool—the world's largest heated salt-water pool with 6.5 million gallons of water—was chilling after closing out another season with performers like Esther Williams and Billy Rose's Aquacades. The *USS San Francisco* was having its bottom scraped at Pearl Harbor, and its crew was absent during the maintenance. When the Japanese bombers struck Pearl Harbor that morning, the heavy cruiser and its men weren't hit.

World War II had begun and San Francisco geared up to play a significant role. Shipyards proliferated all around the Bay Area—39 in total. Ports were mobilized: Fort Mason and Treasure Island, in San Francisco, and Alameda, in Oakland. Forts Baker, Barry, Cronkhite, and Point beefed up security. Bunkers with heavy artillery were scooped out of cliffs up and down the coast. The California State Guard took shifts to watch over the Golden Gate Bridge, and the Navy pegged a seven-mile, six-ton anti-submarine net

USS San Francisco enters San Francisco Bay, December 1942

underneath it. An underground garage at Union Square became one of the city's 30 air raid shelters. Al Capone, along with other convicts at Alcatraz and San Quentin, washed soldiers' laundry and performed other wartime tasks.

Recruiting took place on steamboats in the bay and at the Palace Hotel. GIs prepared for combat, training in classrooms and practicing drills on the parade grounds at the Presidio and at Fleishhacker Pool. They were quartered at the Presidio and parks and playgrounds until more barracks could be built.

Civilians did their bit, too. A major migration of workers flowed in from all parts of the country; more than 240,000 built and repaired Liberty ships and other sea craft in Bay Area shipyards. Since housing was lacking, residents rented out or shared space in rooms, basements, porches, garages, warehouses, and motels. Like the rest of the country, San Franciscans rolled bandages, sold war bonds and collected used metal, rubber, newspapers, and cooking oil, and conducted black outs. To foil enemy planes, they cloaked the city's colorful Victorian houses in battleship gray paint.

Japanese-American citizens enlisted for combat and trained in top-secret translation and interpretation services. Residing in the Western Addition (Fillmore district), San Francisco's Japanese community—including the Hagiwara family—was established and thriving.

In 1894, George Hagiwara's grandfather, Makoto, had been hired to landscape the Japanese Village for the Midwinter Fair in Golden Gate Park. It was the hit of the fair. Makoto made an offer to park superintendant John McLaren, who gleefully awaited the planned destruction of all the fair's venues: If the Japanese Village was made permanent and Makoto could live there, he would manage it. McLaren and the city agreed. Makoto expanded the village from one acre to five, donated many plants and sculptures and renamed it the Japanese Tea Garden. There, he introduced the fortune cookie. (A Chinese firm in Los Angeles also claimed to introduce the cookies and filed suit in the federal Court of Historical Review in 1983. The judge ruled for the Hagiwaras, reviewing evidence that included a fortune cookie message that read "SF Judge who rules for LA Not Very Smart Cookie.")

But on February 19, 1942, President Franklin Roosevelt's Executive Order No. 9066 reversed the fortunes of the Hagiwaras and the Japanese. Posted on storefronts in Nihonmachi (Japantown), the order directed that "all Japanese persons, both alien and non-alien, will be evacuated." General DeWitt—who had already testified to a congressional committee that, "A Jap's a Jap. They are a dangerous element, whether loyal or not"—worked fast to enforce the order. On March 1, he issued his first proclamation. It delineated military zones in California, Oregon, Washington, and Arizona from which the Army would remove all Japanese to what were officially termed "relocation camps."

The Hagiwaras, along with the entire Japanese community, were ordered to turn in their short wave radios, cameras, and guns. They were forced to sell or abandon their houses, businesses, and belongings, and could only bring what they could carry. The Board of Park Commissioners handed the Hagiwaras a "Notice to Quit," which gave them three days to turn over the tea garden. The family shepherded most of the valuable plants over to a friend's nursery for safekeeping. They boarded a Greyhound bus for Tanforan Assembly Center, a racetrack, where they were housed in horse

From left: Makoto Hagiwara and his daughter, 1924; Midwinter Fair's Japanese Village, 1894

stables and thrown-up tarpaper shacks until being evacuated to Camp Topaz in Delta, Utah, where cramped sheetrock and tarpaper "apartments" offered scant insulation against the extreme winter and summer weather. In all, 120,000 Japanese (8,000 of them San Franciscans) were driven from their homes into internment camps for the duration of the war.

Other minorities fared better. Since China was a U.S. ally, the Chinese Exclusion Act was finally repealed in 1943. Five thousand Chinese worked in the shipyards, a formerly forbidden occupation. Chinese women served tea in traditional Chinese dress in the Hagiwara's Japanese Tea Garden, renamed the Oriental Tea Garden. Women of all races were allowed to take jobs since "the boys" were at war; they made up approximately 20 percent of the defense workforce. One black woman, a former housemaid, commented, "Hitler was the one that got us out of the kitchens."

By 1943, the Bay Area served the Pacific Theatre as the top military command port on the West Coast. More than 1.6 million Americans—soldiers, sailors, and civilians such as Red Cross workers—embarked from the Bay Area on 800 troopships. San Francisco's Golden Gate was their last view of the United States. Thirty thousand a month downed a last drink—on the house—at the Top of the Mark bar at the Mark Hopkins Hotel on Nob Hill. (After the war, many GIs returned to the bar to propose marriage and toast anniversaries.) In addition to its premier military standing, San Francisco gained a rep as best "leave" town on the coast with USO dances and shows, tattoo parlors, Playland (a raucous amusement park at the beach), and plenty of bars and burlesque joints among the sights to see.

The *USS San Francisco* saw action in Guadalcanal and was highly decorated, only to be scrapped after the war and lie in a heap in Golden Gate Park. The wings of its signal bridge were preserved, and in 1950 the Navy dedicated a memorial that incorporated them on an observation platform at Land's End. Joe DiMaggio saw no action and returned to six more seasons as an All-Star for the Yankees; he married Marilyn Monroe at San Francisco's City Hall in 1954. Fleishhacker Pool—expensive to heat and underused—deteriorated, and a 1971 storm delivered a final blow after which it was drained and filled with its own broken-up concrete. GIs who sailed back through the Golden Gate were greeted by a sixty-foot-high illuminated sign on Angel Island that said, "Welcome Home, Well Done." With many soldiers as well as civilians deciding to stay, San Francisco's population grew from 634,000 in 1940 to 774,821 in 1950. The War Memorial opposite City Hall saw the signing of the United Nations Charter by fifty countries on June 26, 1945.

The Hagiwaras came back to find the tea garden in ruins. The city broke its contract and would not let them live in their house or manage the property anymore. In 1952, the garden's name was reinstated and the plants transferred during the war were restored upon the death of the Hagiwaras' nursery friend. Today a well-tended Japanese Tea Garden continues to be a popular attraction in Golden Gate Park.

The majority of Japanese returning from the relocation camps did not return to the Western Addition, choosing to move on to the city's Sunset and Richmond districts. Decades later, President Ronald Reagan signed the Civil Liberties Act of 1988, a redress law that officially apologized to all Japanese Americans who were interned. Congress paid each person $20,000. By then, however, many of the older generation were gone.

JOE DIMAGGIO

Giuseppe Paolo DiMaggio, the eighth of nine children and named after his father, was born to Italian immigrant parents. He grew up in North Beach, the city's "Little Italy" then, where his father had a boat and fished for a living. Joe couldn't tolerate the smell of dead fish, but loved baseball. His father hated baseball and repeatedly told him he was "a lazy good-for-nothing." Joe played four seasons for the San Francisco Seals, setting a record 61-game hitting streak. In 1943, at 29, he joined the Army Air Force and became a sergeant. Joe's parents, along with thousands of other Italian and German immigrants, were classified as "enemy aliens." They were required to carry photo ID booklets and restricted from traveling more than five miles from home. The military confiscated Giuseppe DiMaggio Sr.'s boat and barred him from SF Bay, where he had fished for more than forty years.

CHAPTER 22.

MR. SAN FRANCISCO...AND BAGHDAD-BY-THE-BAY: HERB CAEN

1938–1997

"God, I love this town. I loved it before I was born and I'll love it after I'm gone. But when it's time, if I get to heaven, I'm going to say what every San Franciscan says when they get to heaven: 'It ain't bad, but it ain't San Francisco.'"

–Herb Caen

To write about Herb Caen is to tell the tale of a newspaper columnist who became an icon of San Francisco and who wrote just about everything you'd ever want to say about him and his beloved city.

From 1938 to 1997 he composed 1,000 words each morning, seven days a week, for the *San Francisco Chronicle*. Granted, there was time off for a four-year stint in the Air Force during WWII and time away (1950–8) when he switched to the competition and pounded the keys for the *San Francisco Examiner*. But all told, he typed 14,133,000 words worth of columns, many of which he combined to fill 14 books, winning a special Pulitzer Prize in 1997 for his "continuing contribution as a voice and conscience" of San Francisco. Not bad for a Jewish boy born in 1916 to a pool hall operator in Sacramento.

Caen's column head in the *San Francisco Chronicle*

Of course, Caen claimed to have been conceived in San Francisco, since his parents summered there nine months before his birth at the Panama–Pacific Expo in 1915. He beat it back there as soon as he could after graduating from Sacramento High School (where he penned "Corridor Gossip" as Raisin Caen) and covering sports for the *Sacramento Union*. In 1936, he arrived in San Francisco, having landed a job with the *Chronicle* reporting about radio. Two years later, when the paper suspended the column, he proposed a daily "about town" column. His editor accepted and "It's News to Me," (later simplified to "Herb Caen") debuted July 5, 1938.

Subscribing to the rapid-fire "three dot journalism" style of New York columnist Walter Winchell, he inserted ellipses to shift between subjects ... Over the years, there was little that happened in the city that Caen didn't comment on. He could be witty or serious, mundane or high brow, gossipy or newsy as he mused about the weather, the opera, the war (whichever one was current), capital punishment, sports, politics, visiting celebrities, politicians, the cabbie or waitress he just chatted with or his latest lunch companion. On anything and everything San Francisco, which he dubbed Baghdad-by-the-Bay for its many cultures of residents ... Caen separated thoughts and paragraphs with asterisks.

***

On his beat, Caen walked the city streets, imbibing its people, sites, scents, colors, lights, moods. In his column on December 6, 1959, he combined writer's block with his affection for the city:

"Nothing Ever Happens: The reporter looks out the window at the Old Mint across the street, its ledges lined with pigeons, all in a row. He stares at the old men sitting in the Mission St. sun, draped over their crutches, and wonders what they find to talk about. He cocks an ear to the sounds of the City: the siren sounds of a fire engine threading its way down Market, a cop's whistle making the pigeons shift nervously, the sudden scream of a jet.

A story in each sound, elusive and unattainable."

***

Caen coined a host of terms such as beatnik, Beserkeley, and Frisbeetarianism. In the May 12, 1957, column, under "These Things I Like" he observed: "...Grant Ave. in North Beach at night, with lights glowing dimly in shops filled with artsy-craftiness and distracted abstracts-the sandaled shadows shuffling slowly past, boys looking like girls looking like men looking like crazy."

***

On October 4, 1962, after the Giants clinched the pennant he glowed: "A warm golden cloud of affection swept the streets. It wasn't baseball, it wasn't the Giants, it was a common joy possible to share indiscriminately. The people had a winner ... each other."

***

Caen hobnobbed with rich and famous as well as the not-so-rich and not-so-famous. He was aware of his own roots, recounting, "I wasn't one of the boys until they discovered I loved the city. You gotta outlove them. Well I did." On April 24, 1966, his column seethed at the urban strife: "A Kind of Anger: The City is becoming dangerously hardboiled, unsentimental and compartmentalized. The Ins and Outs have never been farther apart, and the Haves couldn't care less about the Have Nots, a sentiment that is returned in spades, redoubled. ... Today the only feeling that people at one end of Fillmore have for those at the other is to hope they don't come any closer."

***

He loved mingling with people in the streets, at the symphony, in the bars, and down by the bay. Day or night, knocking out a column or knocking down Vitamin V—Stoli straight up with a twist of lemon—his antennae were out, picking up the city so he could beam it out in the next day's copy. On October 13, 1968, he reported:

"Two teeny boppers walk by. They pause in front of Maison Mendesolle to light cigarettes, and I detect the cinnamon smell of marijuana. They giggle and walk on in a cloud of pot. Should I call a cop? ... At the bottom of Powell, six young men with shaved heads and bare feet, with yellow robes between, are singing "Hare Krishna" and ringing bells ... The tourists are going crazy, rushing into Woolworth's across the street to buy more film. ... I guess it's a pretty colorful town, all right. And elegant too."

***

He deplored the skyscrapers being erected in the 1970s, denigrating their architects as "Titans of the T Square who have given us such wonders as pyramids with cars, filing cabinets in the sky, vertical ice trays, sixty-story decks of cards." In his May 6, 1973, column he vented:
"...You architects who have visited San Francisco before may wonder where the city has gone. It's here somewhere, cowering behind hills and down alleys that form the new skyline that is almost indistinguishable from Pittsburgh's, Houston's, or Atlanta's."

***

Caen loved his "cool grey city of love" a line he didn't make up but often quoted from George Sterling's 1923 poem of the same name. Here he describes another day and era of people-watching on October 24, 1974:
"Scene: Hallidie Plaza, at the smelly foot of Powell at Market. Usual cast of characters: drummers, bummers, moochers, hootchy-kootchers, freaks, geeks, tourists taking pictures, pickpockets taking tourists, somebody's missing boy walking arm in arm with somebody's lost daughter. Dudes swagger among the prudes, offering everything from a sniff of coke to a stash of the old grasseroo, and trying to look anonymous among all this the plainclothes cops in their fancy duds, inconspicuous as tarantulas on a wedding cake. ... San Fransensual it is."

***

San Franciscans read Herb Caen daily: The *Chronicle* estimated sales would drop 20 percent if they didn't run him. As Caen grew older, and dropped down to five columns a week in 1990, then three columns a week in 1996, the paper ran old columns to fill out the week. Readers liked to appear in his column and liked to send him letters. He always answered, typing all correspondence and columns with two fingers on his "Loyal Royal tripewriter." Once finished, he was off to the now-defunct watering holes that suited him like his brown felt fedora: Jack's, Baldelli's, Ernie's, and Moose's. He dined with any of his large stable of friends: Alfred Hitchcock, Willie Brown, and Wilkes Bashford to drop but a few names. He was the type of guy who hung out with dames—marrying four, the last a year before he died—as well as women and girls.

George Sterling, 1926

As he aged, he acknowledged, "I tend to live in the past because most of my life is there." But his love and concern for his city along with his wit, never diminished. In April 1996, upon receiving the Pulitzer Prize, he referred to it as his "Pullet Surprise." The next month, learning he had inoperable lung cancer (he smoked for forty years but had quit 25 years earlier) he leveled immediately with his readers. A month later, on June 14, 1996, the city honored his 58 years of columns with Herb Caen Day. He was squired in at the head of a motorcade to an assembly of five mayors, plus journalists, actors, sports figures, and other celebrities, as well as 75,000 readers, at the Embarcadero. They celebrated Caen with song and speech, the release of pigeons and balloons, and a flight of antique planes over the bay. A street was dedicated in his name: Herb Caen Way...

When he died a year later, at 80, his will called for fireworks over Aquatic Park in the shape of typewriter. His pal, *New York Times* writer and bureau chief R.W. Apple Jr., wrote in the paper's obituary on Caen, "His enthusiasm over 50 years is unparalleled in a business known for burned-out cases at age 40. His city has shaped him, and he has helped shape his city."

After all is said and done, it's fitting to leave the last words to Caen: "The only thing wrong with immortality is that it tends to go on forever."

CHAPTER 23.

THE BOOKSTORE, THE BEATS, AND THE POETICKALL BOMSHELL: LAWRENCE FERLINGHETTI

1955

"Poets, come out of your closets,
Open your windows, open your doors,
You have been holed up too long in your closed worlds"

 –Lawrence Ferlinghetti from his *Populist Manifesto*

In North Beach on June 3, 1957, Shig Murao, a bearded, be-spectacled bookstore manager in a Pendleton shirt and bowler hat, sold a 75-cent paperback book of poetry to an undercover cop. The officer arrested Murao, along with the owner of the bookstore, Lawrence Ferlinghetti.

Prior to his arrest, Ferlinghetti had lived a full 38 years of life. Months before he was born, in New York, in 1919, his father died; months after, his mother was committed to an insane asylum. His French aunt raised him in France for five years, then brought him to New York City and put him in an orphanage—where he first encountered English—while she looked for work (a common practice at the time for hard-up parents). Ferlinghetti's love for both the French and English languages (and later, Italian) is evident in his illustrious work as a writer, poet, and translator of poems. After serving

as a commander of a submarine chaser in WWII and participating in the Normandy landings, Ferlinghetti earned a master's degree in English from Columbia University in New York, then crossed back to Paris where he was awarded a doctorate with a "mention tres honorable" in poetry from the Sorbonne.

I am waiting for my case to come up
and I am waiting
for a rebirth of wonder
and I am waiting
for someone to really discover America
and wail
-Lawrence Ferlinghetti from "I am Waiting" from his poetry book *A Coney Island of the Mind*

In 1951, Ferlinghetti moved to San Francisco, where he has resided ever since. He taught French to adults, painted, worked for free as an art critic, and translated French poet Jacques Prévert. Peter Martin published the translations in *City Lights*, his short-lived popular culture magazine titled after the Charlie Chaplin film. In 1953, in partnership with Martin—each having put up $500—Ferlinghetti opened the doors of City Lights bookstore. It was unique because it sold highbrow paperbacks, rather than pulp fiction, for 25 to 75 cents. It appealed to literary types, especially beats. To Ferlinghetti, the bookstore was "...not an uptight place but a center for the intellectual community."

Despite giving away books and not prosecuting thieves, City Lights prospered, becoming a major beat hang out. In 1955, taking a $1,000 pay out, Martin re-located to New York to establish a film bookstore. That same year, Ferlinghetti founded City Lights Publishing and printed three books of poetry as part of his Pocket Poet Series, starting with his own.

...and I am waiting
for the discovery
of a new symbolic western frontier
and I am waiting
for the American Eagle
to really spread its wings

and straighten up and fly right
–Lawrence Ferlinghetti from "I am Waiting" from his poetry book *A Coney Island of the Mind*

In late September 1955, posters and postcards went up in San Francisco announcing:

"Six poets at the Six Gallery. Kenneth Rexroth, M.C. Remarkable collection of angels all gathered at once in the same spot. Wine, music, dancing girls, serious poetry, free satori. Small collection for wine and postcards. Charming event."

Poet Gary Snyder wrote his friend, poet Phil Whalen, to hurry down from Oregon for what augured to be a "poetickall Bomshell."

On the evening of October 7, at an art gallery a few blocks from City Lights, 150 beats—including Ferlinghetti—passed around jugs of California Burgundy, forked over dimes and quarters to writer Jack Kerouac to pay for it, and waited for the evening to begin. It was an evening worth waiting for, as it would be a seminal event in beat history, igniting a renaissance of poetry in San Francisco and solidifying it as a beat haven akin to New York City's Greenwich Village.

Kenneth Rexroth, in suspenders, bow tie, and pinstriped suit, was the first poet to stand before the audience in the dim gallery. Revered as an elder and for his weekly literary salons and radio show, Rexroth did not read that night but served as Master of Ceremonies. After making some opening remarks, he introduced the first of the five poets to read that night. Phil Lamantia read the poems of a recently deceased friend; then Michael McClure delivered "For the Death of 100 Whales," a poem of fury at a senseless slaughter by U.S. soldiers; followed by Phil Whalen and his succinct "Plus Ça Change," about an aging couple. Intermission

Jack Kerouac, c. 1956

came next, with what was a palpable feeling of camaraderie and the downing of more wine.

Then Rexroth introduced the organizer of the night's readings, Allen Ginsberg, who had a new poem ready for its first reading. Wearing a work shirt and jeans and showing the effects of the Burgundy, Ginsberg took the floor. Steadying himself, he uttered the first part of "Howl," beginning with its electrifying words, "I saw the best minds of my generation destroyed by madness, starving hysterical naked…"

Allen Ginsberg reads part of his poem 'Howl'' for the first time at the Six Gallery, 1955

It was the howl heard 'round the world. "Howl" was groundbreaking because it took a huge whack at contemporary culture, nakedly exposing one man's pettiness, ire, and desires, and hitting on subjects like sex—hetero and homo—with words that weren't publicly spoken in the 1950s.

The next day Ferlinghetti wired Ginsberg, "I greet you at the beginning of a great literary career," and promised to publish the lengthy poem. *Howl and Other Poems*, City Lights' fourth title, hit the bookstores in September 1956. The squares (non-beats) judged its raw language revolting and resolved to keep its scandalous subjects taboo. Murao and Ferlinghetti were arrested and put on trial for selling obscene material. The *Chronicle* headline stated, "The Cops Don't Allow No Renaissance Here" as the case went national.

and I am waiting
for the Age of Anxiety
to drop dead
and I am waiting
for the war to be fought
which will make the world safe
for anarchy
and I am waiting

for the final withering away
of all governments
–Lawrence Ferlinghetti from "I am Waiting" from his poetry book *A Coney Island of the Mind*

The San Francisco municipal prosecutor categorized the book as pornography due to its "filthy, vulgar, obscene, and disgusting language." The ACLU represented Ferlinghetti and Murao and had prestigious professors and writers testify to *Howl*'s literary merits. After a drawn-out trial, the judge let Murao off early, deciding it was impossible to ascertain if he knew he was selling lewd material. The judge acquitted Ferlinghetti—and, effectively the book—determining that *Howl*, though controversial, possessed redeeming social content. It was a precedent-setting First Amendment case that continues to affect censorship and pornography cases to this day. Ferlinghetti weighed in on the case in a *Chronicle* article, writing, "It is not the poet but what he observes which is revealed as obscene. The great obscene wastes of *Howl* are the sad wastes of the mechanized world, lost among atom bombs and insane nationalisms."

Ginsberg had questioned whether the 1,000 copies that Ferlinghetti had

Allen Ginsberg, Neal Cassady, Lawrence Ferlinghetti, and friends in front of Ferlinghetti's City Lights bookstore, 1956

printed of *Howl* would sell. They did. By the end of the trial *Howl* was in its fourth printing—a 5,000 copy run. It enabled Ginsberg to make a living as a poet and claim his desired career. *Howl* continues to be taught in colleges and read out loud at anniversaries of the 1955 Six Gallery reading. It has sold more than a million copies and never gone out of print.

and I am waiting
for a reconstructed Mayflower
to reach America
with its picture story and tv rights
sold in advance to the natives
and I am waiting
for the lost music to sound again
in the Lost Continent
in a new rebirth of wonder
–Lawrence Ferlinghetti from "I am Waiting" from his poetry book *A Coney Island of the Mind*

In 1958, Ferlinghetti published his book of poems, *A Coney Island of the Mind*, which continues to be a bestseller today. He has been honored with a slew of awards for his books, poems, and political activism, and he reigned as San Francisco's poet laureate for 1998. City Lights Publishers continues to print the works of writers and poets from around the world. In 2001, the Board of Supervisors designated City Lights a local landmark for its "seminal role in the literary and cultural development of San Francisco and the nation … for championing First Amendment protections, and for publishing and giving voice to writers and artists everywhere."

BEATS DEFINE BEAT

"The point of beat is that you get beaten down to a certain nakedness where you are actually able to see the world in a visionary way which is the old classical understanding of what happens in the dark night of the soul."
-Allen Ginsberg, beat poet

"Members of the generation that came of age after World War II, who supposedly, as a result of disillusionment stemming from the cold war, espouse mystical detachment, and relaxation of social and sexual tensions."
-Jack Kerouac, author of *On the Road*, *The Dharma Bums*, *Big Sur*, and other beat novels.

CHAPTER 24.

WESTERN ADDITION AND SUBTRACTION: MARY ROGERS AND JUSTIN HERMAN

1960s

When 40-year-old Mary Helen Rogers moved into the Fillmore in 1965 with her husband, Sergeant Melvin Rogers, and their twelve children, she only thought of it as the main district in San Francisco that would rent to black families. But the move placed her at the center of an historic neighborhood, and the battle to save it.

Nearly one hundred years earlier, a new district opened up west of Van Ness—the Western Addition. It was a white, middle-class area—a suburb with farms and Painted Ladies (ornate Victorian-style houses)—that the city enveloped over time. In 1906, it was one of the few areas to survive the earthquake and fires. Its single-family Victorians became boarding houses and displaced people from different parts of the city moved in. Fillmore Street, a cobblestone road named after Millard Fillmore, the president at statehood, became the district's main commercial thoroughfare, so dominant that people said "The Fillmore" when referring to the district.

Starting in the 1920s, for decades people strutted the street at night in their furs and finery. They enjoyed dances, balls, talent contests, and jazz

Fillmore Street, 1960s. From left: Pony Poindexter, John Coltrane and Frank Fisher jamming at Jimbo's Bop City, c. 1950

clubs—The New Orleans Swing Club, Jimbo's Bop City, Jackson's Nook, the Long Bar, the Blue Mirror, and Club Alabam to list but a few. Ella, Etta, Billie, Louis, Trane, Monk, The Count, The Duke—all the greats—played them, earning the Fillmore the title of the "Harlem of the West."

WWII resulted in a cultural makeover of the Western Addition. The number of African Americans sextupled, from 5,000 in 1935 to 30,000 in 1945. Forced into internment camps, the Japanese population dropped to zero. Once released, the Japanese relocated to the Sunset and Richmond districts, which were closed to the likes of Mary Rogers. By the 1950s, absentee landlords owned 90 percent of the Western Addition and The Painted Ladies were sagging—denied the cosmetic and structural infusions needed to keep them from withering into untenable relics.

Enter the San Francisco Redevelopment Agency. Founded in 1948 as part of a national program to modernize, in 1954 the Agency introduced the term "urban renewal," defining it as slum removal and renovation. Redevelopment agencies across the country began excising urban neighborhoods, (where 75 percent of the inhabitants were working-class minorities) and replacing the blighted blocks with new roads and buildings for new inhabitants (usually middle class or wealthier whites). The San Francisco agency selected the Western Addition for what would become one of the West's largest urban renewal projects, affecting hundreds of city blocks and nearly 20,000 residents. In 1960, the mayor hired Justin Herman, a city planner, to head the agency.

Coming on the scene in 1965, Rogers recollected, "I was appalled at the housing situation in San Francisco and really got angry when I found out that nobody wanted to rent to black families. I tried to rent a house in the Sunset and when they found out I was black, all of a sudden it was rented. I had to move to Webster Street between Eddy and Ellis [in the Western Addition], in one of the worst vice communities you could move into."

By the time Rogers and her family moved in, Phase 1 of the Western Addition renewal plan, labeled "A-1", was in full swing. Herman used eminent domain to demolish the homes of families, some of whom had lived in them close to a century. He erected the Japanese Culture and Trade Center, a shopping center, which displaced 6,000 people. A new saying circulated in the old neighborhood: "Urban renewal = Negro removal." Also in the early 1960s, four-lane Geary Street was renovated into eight-lane Geary Expressway, which tunneled under Fillmore Street. The new expressway speeded traffic from downtown to the west side and bisected the neighborhood, separating the black blocks of the Fillmore from its recently re-established Japanese community, and from the wealthy whites up the hill in Pacific Heights.

Rogers got busy improving her community, volunteering at her children's school and helping create WACO (Western Addition Community Organization) in 1966. "We saw that kids got back in school, that mothers got their welfare grants on time, and cleaned up the streets with brooms and shovels."

Mary Rogers and Justin Herman

Moving a Victorian house, c. 1970s

Herman was equally busy ramping up Phase 2—"Western Addition A-2"—a more ambitious project that impacted 64 blocks and 14,000 residents. Unlike A-1, which bulldozed all buildings, A-2 promised to destroy some dilapidated Victorian houses and restore others. It would also compensate ejected renters and homeowners financially and issue "Certificates of Preference" to dislocated businesses. Rogers echoed the view of the majority, contending that the Redevelopment Agency's "bottom line was to remove all blacks out of the Western Addition, build high-rise and high-income apartments, and bring all the suburbanites to San Francisco." Her response? "I refused to accept that I couldn't stay where I wanted to stay. I refused to go somewhere else because I was black. I decided I wasn't going to move. I wasn't going anywhere until I got good and ready."

WACO got active, spreading the word, picketing, and filing suits for compensation. "We wanted to still be a part of the community. We wanted our businesses to still exist. Our churches to still exist. Our children to still go to the neighborhood schools," Rogers explained. WACO applied to the Redevelopment Agency for funds to help businesses but was rebuffed. The agency performed studies and then, Rogers states, "They took all of those stores and emptied the land and tore all of those buildings down."

The agency's brochure called for "more socially oriented housing for the Western Addition A-2 project area." While some moderate and low-income housing was built, it took years—decades in some cases—to secure funds and build the new buildings. To add insult to injury, gentrification took place as decrepit Painted Ladies were revived by new, well-heeled homeowners. (Some of these houses are located in Alamo Square, recognizable from the opening credits of the TV show *Full House*.)

WACO sued the agency. Reverend Hannibal Williams, co-founder of WACO, summed up the results: "We didn't win an all-out victory but we stopped two parts of the process: we stopped demolition and we stopped the acquisition of homes. ... We slowed the agency down, but in the end, urban renewal became what we feared it would: it became black removal." Like many, he believed that, "Justin Herman literally destroyed the neighborhood."

In 1971, after 11 years as director of the Redevelopment Agency, Herman dropped dead of a heart attack. The next year Justin Herman Plaza in the Embarcadero was dedicated. Mary Rogers went on to be the community relations manager of the Housing Authority for 20 years, and to receive the Rosa Parks Award for community service. She died in 2006, and in 2012 was honored at City Hall at the annual Juneteenth celebration (commemorating the announcement of the abolition of slavery on June 19, 1865). Rogers was remembered for her activism as the "Mother of the Fillmore."

Many lessons were learned from the redevelopment of the Western Addition, primarily that urban renewal programs must consult and engage all communities involved and allocate sufficient funds to reach their goals. Willie Brown, who arrived in the Fillmore in 1951 at age 17, and in 1996 became the city's first black mayor, summed up the tragedy best: "It was a devastating blow to African Americans in San Francisco, a blow from which we, frankly, have never really recovered. There is no true African-American community comparable to what was the Fillmore. This great life, that was comparable to the Harlem Renaissance, was destroyed by the redevelopment process."

Today there is a concerted movement to create a Jazz Historic District. New venues are appearing in the Western Addition, notably Yoshi's in the Fillmore Heritage Center, where Japanese food and jazz are served up every night.

THE FREEWAY REVOLT

Mayor John Shelley

A corollary to urban re-development was the proposed construction of new highways in and around U.S. cities in the 1950s and '60s. San Francisco's Planning Commission put forth the "Trafficways Plan" to unclog traffic around the city with nine express roadways. Citizens reacted, initiating what was termed the "Freeway Revolt." They argued that by crisscrossing the city, the roads would cut off neighborhoods and spoil the city's beauty and cohesion.

The emergence of the Embarcadero Freeway, an elevated eyesore that ran from the Bay Bridge to the wharf area, blocking the view of the Bay, in 1955 didn't help the commission's case. Columnist Herb Caen referred to it as the "Dambarcadero." The Central Freeway, an elevated expressway, was also partially constructed, turning Hayes Valley in the Western Addition into a rundown, crime-ridden area.

Much of the Trafficways Plan was scrapped as the Freeway Revolt spurred resident resistance and politicians joined in. In 1966, Mayor John Shelley declared, "There will be a freeway on the moon before we get one in San Francisco." Nature weighed in with the 1989 Loma Prieta 'quake, which collapsed enough of the Embarcadero and Central freeways that the former was completely demolished and the Hayes Valley section of the latter was taken down, reviving the neighborhood.

The Painted Ladies at Alamo Square in Western Addition

CHAPTER 25.

THE BLOSSOMING OF FLOWER POWER: BEHIND THE SCENE WITH BILL GRAHAM

1960s

"The '60s were a leap in human consciousness. Mahatma Gandhi, Malcolm X, Martin Luther King, Che Guevara, they led a revolution of conscience. The Beatles, The Doors, Jimi Hendrix created revolution and evolution themes. The music was like Dalí, with many colors and revolutionary ways."

–Carlos Santana

In the dead of night in the mid 1960s, a man in his 30s whisked around the city on a 1956 Lambretta scooter. He stopped frequently to stick up psychedelic posters that announce The Doors, Moby Grape, The Mothers of Invention—the next band to play the Fillmore. To find his life's passion, Bill Graham had endured many more challenging roads than San Francisco's hills.

Wolfgang Grajonca (anglicized to Bill Graham) was born in 1931 to middle-class Jewish parents in Berlin. His father, a civil engineer, died two days after he was born from blood poisoning caused by a work accident. His mother supported Graham and his five sisters by selling flowers and skirts at the market. To safeguard them from rising Nazism, she put Graham

BILL GRAHAM PRESENTS IN SAN FRANCISCO

JEFFERSON AIRPLANE
GRATEFUL DEAD
FRI. 12 AUG.
SAT. 13 AUG.
FILLMORE AUDITORIUM

TICKETS   "GRATEFUL DEAD" Photo by Herb Greene

San Francisco Mime Troupe, 1967

and his youngest sister, Tolla, in a kinderheim—a boarding school. His remaining four sisters escaped Hitler's machine, but his mother was gassed on a train en route to Auschwitz. Graham and Tolla were moved to safety in France until Germany occupied it and they were sent on a grueling cross-country march to freedom with 62 other children. When Tolla got pneumonia and was hospitalized, Red Cross workers told Graham to continue marching with the group. Tolla was never heard from again. Of the 64 children, only 11 survived. Graham sailed into New York in 1941 weighing 55 pounds and suffering from malnutrition and rickets. He was adopted and eventually earned a business degree from City College and served in the Korean War. After a dozen years, he reunited with his four surviving sisters.

By the early 1960s, Graham had knocked around a bit. He'd worked the Borscht Belt hotels in the Catskills as a server, maître d', and poker host; been a cabbie and champion mambo dancer in Manhattan; acted bit parts in Hollywood; and held a dozen other jobs from New York to California. Living in San Francisco near his only sister in the U.S., he was adrift and he knew it. He took a job with the San Francisco Mime Troupe as a business manager, doing everything from ticketing to truck driving to striking the set. He kept away from the troupe's productions and radical politics—neither of which he fully supported. One afternoon, the troupe was performing in Lafayette Park when leader Ronny Davis was busted for obscenity. Already crashing financially, the Mime Troupe needed cash—fast.

On November 6, 1965, Graham put on his first benefit—an "appeal party" for the Mime Troupe—in a loft in the skid row district south of Market. Graham had a crude stage set up, along with some basic lights, and implemented a sliding scale entrance fee, ranging from $1 to $48. Despite the low price, Graham and the Mime Troupe didn't expect much. There'd been other fundraisers that scored low. But they didn't have Graham's unique line-up:

poets Lawrence Ferlinghetti, Michael McClure, and Allen Ginsberg; blues singer John Handy; and rockers The Fugs and Jefferson Airplane. Spotting the long line of people queued up for the benefit was an epiphany for Graham. His excitement grew as he watched these strangers groove with the performers until seven the next morning. Then he totaled the results: The loft held 500 people and 1,500 showed up; they had scored $4,200—a fortune!

"This is the business of the future," Graham declared. It certainly was the start of his true career. "I realized what I wanted to do. Living theater. Taking music and the newborn visual arts and making all of that available in a comfortable surrounding so it would be conducive to open expression. What I saw was that when all this truly worked, that space was magic."

He parted ways with the Mime Troupe over philosophical differences and began booking singers and groups into the Fillmore, a ballroom he leased. Graham added strobe lights and a mirror ball and served free apples but no alcohol—grass and psychedelics were the drugs of choice. He commissioned artists to design psychedelic posters—prized collectibles today—and zoomed around on his scooter to post them on walls around the city. He sold tickets; cleaned the bathrooms; interacted with the audience and performers; and battled with cops, politicians, and the rabbi next door to keep the rock rolling. "What I remember about the early shows is that I made notes. ... Hundreds of notes about people coming in, access and egress," Graham recalled. "I was always looking for ways to make the place more haimish (like home)."

Bill Graham, 1974, and the Fillmore

Jimi Hendrix, 1967, and Janis Joplin

The Fillmore became the place to trip the strobe lights fantastic as Graham brought in the greats. One night you could groove to The Doors, another night hear Janis belt out the blues, another be mellow with Otis Redding; it was an Escher landscape of new vistas. In halls illuminated with black light, people showed up to dance communally, try new substances, and create a new world with new music. Graham was there to help make it possible. He hired a panoply of stars (rising and fixed), including Jimi Hendrix, Muddy Waters, and Sly and the Family Stone, and began managing groups such as Jefferson Airplane and Santana.

The Fillmore's rise reverberated in a larger cultural transformation erupting in the city. On January 14, 1967, Graham was on the scene at the polo field in Golden Gate Park for a happening that the Berkeley Barb proclaimed would "shower the country with waves of ecstasy and purification" and forge "a union of love and activism" according to the *San Francisco Oracle*.

The Human Be-In, (full name: "A Gathering of the Tribes for a Human Be-In"), was a watershed event. Triggered by a law making LSD illegal, the event brought together 30,000 hippies; yippies (Jerry Rubin and his Youth International Party); diggers; radicals; teenyboppers; poets; Zen Buddhists; and local bands Big Brother and the Holding Company, Quicksilver

Messenger Service, and the Grateful Dead. People sold handmade sandals, beads, tie-died clothing, patchouli oil, and crystals. The "chemist"—"Bear" Owsley Stanley—brought a batch of white lightening (LSD). Timothy Leary famously exhorted the crowd to "Turn on, tune in, and drop out," Allen Ginsberg and Ram Dass chanted mantras, Gary Snyder and Michael McClure read poetry, Dick Gregory fused politics and comedy, and Hells Angels rounded up lost children. People danced, sang, played tambourines, flutes, and bongos, made love, took drugs, affirmed their anti-war beliefs, and above all, came together.

"Before [the Be-In] there seemed to be about twenty of us. ... Suddenly there were thousands ... and we felt this tremendous strength in numbers. No one was trying to do any damage to anyone else, and there was a real sense that we all coexisted in as near perfect harmony as human beings are capable of." Paul Kantner, Jefferson Airplane

The Be-In set off a rush of youth to Haight-Ashbury for its drug-taking counterculture and cheap rents. Mayor John Shelley went to the Board of Supervisors, stating that he vehemently discouraged the "... summer influx of indigent young people who ... believe that their vagrant presence will be tolerated in the city, particularly in the Haight-Ashbury district." Young people across the country ignored him. The "Summer of Love" saw the Haight's population surge from 7,000 to 75,000. It was the largest youth migration in U.S. history and a gold rush of sorts, only this time the quest was for freedom, good vibes, and perhaps a little gold—Acapulco Gold marijuana, not the precious metal.

As dropouts and runaways flocked to the city, a parallel surge occurred in crime and drug and housing problems. Graham started enlisting the Haight Ashbury Free Clinic for medical aid at outdoor concerts. He also opened Fillmore East in New York City and re-branded the original

The Human Be-In at Golden Gate Park, January 1967

The Doors at the Fillmore Auditorium, late 1960s

as Fillmore West. But the scene in San Francisco kept transforming, as hippies and other counterculture types were stereotyped and simultaneously exploited in the media, infiltrated and attacked by law enforcement, and misunderstood and put down by mainstream culture. Still, the kids kept coming and the times kept a-changing, with San Francisco an epicenter of the transformation—a legendary city with the legendary sound and culture.

The legacy of the hippies, counterculturists, and political activists continues to be denied, castigated, celebrated, and pondered. Graham's legacy is easier. He went on to produce more groups, concerts, and benefits, and cement a reputation as a pioneering promoter. He died in 1991, in a helicopter crash just north of the Bay Area, after signing Huey Lewis and the News for a concert benefitting victims of the 1989 Oakland hills fire. A week later, close to 500,000 people again swarmed the polo field in Golden Gate Park for "Laughter, Love, and Music," an eight-hour free concert to honor Graham. Santana; Joan Baez; Neil Young; and Crosby, Stills, and Nash played their respects. As Robert Greenfield wrote in *Bill Graham Presents: My Life Inside Rock and Out*, the autobiography he co-authored with Graham: "For the first time ever, all those many people had turned out for a man who played no instrument. Who could not really sing. Who had not written a single word of any song performed from the stage that day. At long last, the crowd had finally come for Bill."

THE SAN FRANCISCO MIME TROUPE

The Mime Troupe combines satire, song, and costumes with extensive research to reach people from all walks of life. The troupe has staged their plays for free or a small donation in parks and venues in San Francisco and around the world since 1959. Check www.sfmt.org for performances.

HAIGHT ASHBURY FREE CLINIC

To deal with the medical needs of incoming hippies and the indifference of established hospitals, medical intern David Smith opened the clinic on June 9, 1967. The first free clinic in the country, it continues to serve the community and includes a Bill Graham Center on its premises.

HUCKLEBERRY'S FOR RUNAWAYS

Named after Huck Finn by its founder, Methodist minister Ted McIlvenna, Huckleberry's was created to shelter youths arriving in the summer of 1967. It carries on today as a multiservice youth agency and wellness center.

CHAPTER 26.

THE RISE OF THE CASTRO AND HARVEY MILK

1970s

"We will not win our rights by staying quietly in our closets...We are coming out to fight the lies, the myths, the distortions. We are coming out to tell the truths about gays, for I am tired of the conspiracy of silence."

–Harvey Milk

Starting the late 1940s, gays and lesbians were arrested as "inmates of a disorderly house" and carted off in police wagons for holding hands or dancing together or simply being in a gay bar or attending a private party. Even if the charges didn't stick, their names were published in the newspaper, causing many to lose their jobs or even their families. Sick of this routine harassment, and wanting a place to convene for socializing, lesbians and gay men in San Francisco began to organize. In 1952, Hal Call started a local branch of the Mattachine Society, an early gay rights organization, and in 1955 a couple, Phyllis Lyon and Del Martin, founded Daughters of Bilitis (DOB), the country's first lesbian organization. Both organizations met secretly and attracted a few hundred brave souls.

By 1969, when Harvey Milk arrived on the scene, police raids were less

Castro and Market streets, 1944

frequent, but bars still had to pay off cops to allow dancing. Meanwhile, liberal politicians were paying attention to the rising politically active gay community, which was forming new organizations. Milk showed up as another budding longhair, bounding away from his conservative views and closeted gay lifestyle in New York. Born in 1930 to middle-class Jewish parents, he'd grown up on Long Island. He graduated from SUNY Albany, where he studied math and history. He appeared friendly and gregarious, but hid his sexual orientation—a secret he kept during his three years in the Navy. By 1969, when his lover Scott Smith's job as stage manager for a musical touring company took them to San Francisco, he was ready.

It was apt that the musical was *Hair*. Milk landed a job with an investment firm downtown, but was fired when he refused to cut his hair. Smith and Milk settled in the sunny Eureka Valley district, for decades a working-class area dominated by Irish Catholics, Germans and Scandinavians. By the early 1970s, most of these blue-collar workers had taken off for the 'burbs, either because their jobs moved or they were alarmed at the incursion of the first gay bar. They vacated rundown Italianate Edwardian houses with cheap rents, which appealed to gay men like Milk and Smith. The couple rented a place on the main drag, the street that gave the district its new name: Castro.

In 1973, Milk and Smith opened Castro Camera and occupied the apartment above it. The store barely sustained them, so when a state taxman came knocking for a $100 advance payment, Milk was ticked off. He raged over the payment (and eventually got it reduced to $30); he raged over the deceitful, self-serving testimony of government officials at the Watergate hearings; and he raged over city funds going to tourism and developers, instead of teachers and other underdogs. Out of this crucible of outrage emerged a decision that set the course of the rest of his life: He would plunge into politics and try to change things.

First, he earned the allegiance of the Teamsters Union, which was boycotting six beer companies for not hiring union truck drivers. Milk persuaded the gay bars to stop ordering the companies' beer

Milk supporters display their enthusiasm, 1975

in exchange for the union hiring more gay drivers. It was a success. All companies signed a union contract except one, Coors. Gay bars continued the boycott of Coors for years. Second, he made coalitions with gay and straight business owners for the first Castro Street Fair. Third, he ran for city supervisor. Milk spoke to a wide variety of groups and worked the press, all while sporting a ponytail and beard, and lacking staff, funds, and endorsements. He lost, but did unexpectedly well, chalking up 16,700 votes to come in tenth out of thirty-two candidates, and proving that the gay vote was something to reckon with.

Exchanging his hippie look for a secondhand three-piece suit and a shave, Milk ran again in 1975. Six supe seats were vacant. He came in seventh, missing a seat by one. But he gained endorsements and forged new alliances, especially with George Moscone, the new mayor. In 1976, Moscone appointed him to the Board of Appeals, making Milk the first openly gay city commissioner in the U.S. After five months, Moscone fired him. Milk was running for a state assembly seat and the city's rules forbade holding an office and running for one simultaneously. He accepted help from Reverend Jim Jones' People's Temple members—as did his opponent—but warned his volunteers to always treat them nicely because "they're dangerous and you never want to be on their bad side." Milk ran as underdog, enduring bomb threats and menacing letters. Still he nearly pulled it off, losing by a little more than 10 percent.

In 1976, Christian fundamentalist Anita Bryant began her "Save Our Children" campaign to repeal a Dade County, Florida, ordinance, banning

Harvey Milk in San Francisco's seventh annual gay freedom parade on Market Street on June 26, 1978

discrimination based on sexual orientation. Contending "homosexuals cannot biologically reproduce children; therefore, they must recruit our children," Bryant spearheaded a hate campaign that resulted in the murders of gays across the country (including in San Francisco), the entry of the word "homophobia" into the lexicon, and a 2:1 vote for repeal. Other counties across the country soon followed suit, putting anti-discrimination laws out to the electorate, which voted for repeal.

Against this backdrop, Milk stepped forward once again, and made his third run for city supervisor in 1977. Working in his favor was the change of many heterosexuals' hearts due to Bryant's vitriolic crusade, as well as the influx of nearly 30,000 gays to the Castro. Additionally, a re-districting measure that Milk had pushed for the year before had passed. The Castro district was his; he beat out 16 other hopefuls to win by 30 percent.

On January 8, 1978, arm-in-arm with his beloved and trailed by 150 supporters, Milk walked the fifteen blocks from Castro Camera to City Hall to claim his office.

As supervisor, Milk sponsored a civil rights bill that made discrimination based on sexual orientation illegal. It passed ten to one. The lone dissenter was Supervisor Dan White, a former firefighter and cop who represented police and other working-class conservatives. Mayor Moscone proudly signed the bill, and Milk moved onto other issues, opposing the closing of an elementary school in his district and pushing a pooper-scooper ordinance that required pet owners to clean up after their pooches or be fined.

That same year, building on Anita Bryant and hoping it would boost his chances to be elected governor of California, Assemblyman John Briggs put a proposition on the state ballot. If passed, Prop 6 would ban homosexuals from teaching in public schools, and legalize the termination of any educator "advocating, imposing, encouraging or promoting" homosexuality. An early poll showed Prop 6 winning by 61 percent. Partnering with activist-professor Sally Gearhart, Milk debated Briggs all over the state. Briggs claimed, "If [homosexuals] don't recruit children or very young people, they'd all die away. ... That's why they want to be teachers." Urging gays and lesbians to stop living invisible lives and come out, Milk quipped, "If it were true that children mimicked their teachers, you'd sure have a helluva lot more nuns running around."

On November 7, Prop 6 went down to major defeat and so did Briggs. There was dancing and celebrating in the Castro. Three days later, Milk celebrated again. Dan White had quit. While they had had a cordial relationship, after Milk's support of a mental health facility for troubled teens in White's district, White barely spoke to Milk.

On November 18, Jim Jones led his temple of 914 people into mass suicide. The day before, White changed his mind and asked Mayor Moscone for his job back. At first, Moscone was inclined to tear up White's resignation letter, but then stood fast. On November 27, the mayor was scheduled to announce White's replacement. That morning, after evading metal detectors by entering through the basement, White walked up City Hall's grand staircase to Moscone's office. Seeking to mollify a shouting White, the mayor escorted him to his inner office. White pulled out a revolver and shot him twice. Moscone fell to the floor, and White moved close to deliver two final shots to his head. After reloading—this time with hollow-point bullets—White rushed out into the hall, then invited Milk into his former office.

San Francisco Examiner, November 28, 1978

When they were inside, he fired two bullets at Milk, who crumpled to his knees. Once again White closed in, sending his last three bullets into the back of Milk's head.

That night, 40,000 people, holding candles, repeated Milk's victory procession by walking silently from the Castro to City Hall. There were speeches, and Joan Baez sang. The next day the two bodies lay in state in City Hall's rotunda and flags flew at half mast. After services at City Hall, a temple, and the Opera House, Milk's ashes were scattered in the bay.

Since childhood, Milk had felt he would die prematurely. Motivated by the death threats received during his campaigns, he taped three recordings in 1977 to be played in case he should be assassinated. In them he enunciated his thoughts, desires, and wishes, naming his preferred successors and saying, "If a bullet should enter my brain, let that bullet destroy every closet door."

Due to poor prosecution and a shrewd counsel (who originated the famous "Twinkie defense," blaming White's crimes on his junk food consumption),

Demonstrations following the controversial sentencing of Dan White for the assassinations of Mayor George Moscone and Supervisor Harvey Milk, 1979

White was convicted of only manslaughter. He served five years before hanging himself at home in his garage in 1985.

Meanwhile, the Yerba Buena Center was renamed the Moscone Center. Martin and Lyon continued their work for women's rights for more than 50 years. In 2008 they became the city's first same-sex couple to be married legally by Mayor Gavin Newsome. Milk has been memorialized in many ways, including having a plaza in the Castro and a high school for LGBTQ students in New York named after him.

In 2009, Governor Arnold Schwarzenegger designated May 22—Milk's birthday—as Harvey Milk Day. That same year, President Barack Obama awarded Milk the

Phyllis Lyon and Del Martin, founders of the Daughters of Bilitis, c. 1970

Presidential Medal of Freedom, affirming, "He fought discrimination with visionary courage and conviction."

CHAPTER 27.

A MATTER OF HABIT IN THE TIME OF AIDS

1980s

In 1965, a 21-year-old man with the muscled body of a trained dancer left his family in Oregon for San Francisco. Ken Horne was full of hope and dreams. The theater tantalized him with its sets, costumes, and romantic stories; he desired everything about the ballet, especially to be adored by an audience as he danced. He began taking classes at the San Francisco Ballet School. And meeting men. He felt he'd arrived, he told friends, like Cinderella at the ball.

On Easter Sunday 1979, three men appeared on Castro Street wearing nuns' habits for what turned into "an afternoon of revelation and retribution" according to one of them, Sister Rumi Sufi Heart Now. By 1980, they officially formed their order—the Sisters of Perpetual Indulgence—and had hand-sewn habits modeled after those worn by Belgian nuns in the 1300s. With their wimples and white make-up, The Sisters of Perpetual Indulgence were more than drag queens in nun attire. They showed chest hair and rollerskated while they parodied the Catholic Church and its imagery. And, like the nuns they emulated, they served their community by devoting themselves to its political, spiritual, and charitable needs.

By 1980 Ken Horne had lost sight of a dance career. In 1969 he'd opted for a clerical job with BART (Bay Area Rapid Transit) and ascended to station manager. It was a day job that afforded him a night life. By now he was wearing leather and hitting the hardcore bars, having suspended his search for "Mr. Right," and content with for "Mr. Right for the Night."

In August 1980, the Sisters showed up at the annual Castro Street Fair (usually held in October), founded by slain supervisor Harvey Milk in 1974. If Ken Horne had wanted to attend, his body wouldn't let him. He was feeling lousy and had been forced to go on disability, too rundown to do his job. Horne started seeing a therapist and resolved to take his life back. On November 25, he dragged himself to dermatologist James Groundwater. Horne told the doctor that he'd been feeling ill for two years and ticked off his symptoms: fatigue, nausea, diarrhea, and now these blue-purple spots—lesions—on his thigh and chest.

"My life is falling apart. What's happening to me?" he fretted. Groundwater took his blood, and performed a series of needle-prick skin tests and told him to make a follow-up appointment.

Ten days later, Horne returned. In his 26 years of practice, Groundwater had never seen results like these. The blood tests showed something was out of whack with Horne's white blood cells. More mystifying, the skin tests indicated his immune system was acting abnormally. Horne was sicker, with two new purple lesions on his chest and more desperate and demanding. Noticing that Horne's lymph nodes were still swollen, Groundwater biopsied them and drew more blood, instructing the lab to test it for all viral diseases. There must be a known cause, he reasoned.

Over the next few months, Horne's condition worsened. Fevers and increasingly severe headaches dominated his

Castro Street scene 1970s

Castro Street Fair, late 1970s

life, and now his eyes were being pummeled with pain, exacerbated by any movement. He wanted answers, but Groundwater was increasingly baffled, as were all the doctors and pathologists he consulted about the case. "He was angry at us because we couldn't find out what the heck was going on with him," Groundwater reflected. Groundwater was certain that the lesions that kept emerging on Horne's body weren't benign, but as hard as he looked, he couldn't find the cause.

On March 30, 1981, Groundwater admitted Horne to the hospital. More specialists examined him. A lumbar puncture revealed cryptococcosis—a fungal infection, and another piece that didn't fill in the puzzle. Ten days later, Horne finally got a diagnosis. A biopsy of a lesion revealed Kaposi's sarcoma (KS). This deepened the mystery, as KS was a skin cancer associated with Eastern European men and normally not fatal. Yet Horne was critically ill and would die if Groundwater couldn't get some answers.

By that time, the Sisters of Perpetual Indulgence were on their way to becoming a 600-member organization with houses, orders, and missions in ten countries. They had a mission statement, "The Sisters of Perpetual Indulgence is a leading-edge Order of queer nuns. .... We believe all people have a right to express their unique joy and beauty and we use humor and irreverent wit to expose the forces of bigotry, complacency and guilt that chain the human spirit."

Those interested in making the lifelong commitment to joining an order and becoming a sister are required to pass through stages from Aspirant to Postulant to Novice to finally be voted in to Fully Professed status. Postulants are allowed to deck themselves out in "festive garb that fits in with Order" (a Catholic school girl's uniform for example). Novices may wear a white veil and the white face make-up but only the Fully Professed have full membership rights, take the black veil and don a habit. Members assign themselves a variety of irreverent names such as Sister Homo Celestial, Sister Rhoda Kill, Sister Eve Volution and so on. Sister Irma Geddon illuminates the philosophy, "The lightness of everything, in addition to the whiteface and the nun's habits, are a mechanism to reach out to people. When we're dressed up like that, kind of like sacred clowns, it allows people to interact with us."

Ken Horne battled with his illness for a year. Having lost his fight to stay at

Sister Boom Boom and other members of The Sisters of Perpetual Indulgence hold an "exorcism" in Union Square during the 1984 Democratic National Convention

home, in November 1981, he was in the hospital relinquishing his life to this still undiagnosed disease. His daily temperature was 102 degrees, his weight was an emaciated 122 pounds, he was blind, he had dementia, and his lungs' work had been taken over by a ventilator. His suffering ceased on November 30. He died not knowing that his KS diagnosis was sent to the CDC (Centers for Disease Control), leading directly to the discovery of the disease that was labeled AIDS (acquired immunodeficiency syndrome) in July 1982.

Play Fair, 1981

"...Violence simmers just below the surface of this city that dances on the edge of the world with gay abandon and abandoned gays. The killing fields around us, alive, sick, dying, and the band is playing louder and faster..."
    –Herb Caen, September 25, 1988, in the *San Francisco Chronicle*

According to the San Francisco Department of Public Health, the "HIV/AIDS epidemic struck SF's gay male community harder than any community in the world." The death toll rose during the 1980s, as 22,602 AIDS cases were reported from 1980 to 1995; 91 percent were gay men—20,530 deaths out of an estimated population of 58,000 gay men. In 1982, the city allocated $1 million for AIDS education and in 1983 the city's AIDS budget exceeded the National Institute of Health's extramural AIDS research budget for the country. In the ensuing years as the rest of the country experienced the ravages of AIDS, funds for prevention and treatment increased.

But in 1981, when federal funds were scant The Sisters of Perpetual Indulgence put on what they maintain was the first-ever AIDS fundraiser. The following year Sister Florence Nightmare, an RN, produced a pamphlet titled "Play Fair." It was one of the first guides to safe sex, and the Sisters continue to distribute it today. In addition, Sisters participated in the Names Project, which began in San Francisco in 1987.

To remember all those lost to AIDS, the NAMES Project created the AIDS Memorial Quilt which is comprised of 3-by-6-foot panels sewn by the deceased's loved ones. With 1.3 million square feet of over 94,000 panels and chapters around the globe, the quilt is the world's largest community art project and was nominated for a Nobel Peace Prize in 1989. The quilt has been seen by more than 18 million people and garnered $4 million in donations. You can see a few quilt panels at Grace Cathedral on Nob Hill and view all panels digitally at www.aidsquilt.org. There is a panel for Ken Horne.

WHERE HAVE ALL THE GRAVEYARDS GONE?
GONE TO COLMA EVERY ONE

When a Sister of Perpetual Indulgence dies, she is considered to have passed through the veil and ascended to become a Nun of the Above. Nun's Rock at AIDS Memorial Grove in Golden Gate Park also commemorates fallen sisters. However, most San Franciscans are not buried in the city.

In 1902 San Francisco ran out of space for cemeteries and outlawed all internments. Ten years later the bodies from graveyards all over the city were disinterred and transferred to Colma, a small town to the south. Today Colma is home to more than 1,400 residents and 1.5 million souls and its cheerful motto is "It's great to be alive in Colma." A few of its famous underground residents are Levi Strauss, Wyatt Earp, Emperor Norton, Adolph Sutro, Makoto Hagiwara, "Doc" Arthur Barker (of the Barker gang, who died during a shoot out while trying to escape Alcatraz), George Moscone, Joe DiMaggio, and Bill Graham.

AIDS Memorial Quilt

CHAPTER 28.

THE NEW ARGONAUTS: DIGGING FOR GOLD ON THE INTERNET

1990s–PRESENT

"In a cavern in a canyon, excavating for a mine,
Lived a miner, 49'er..."

"At a desktop, in a start-up, tapping keys for a new world,
Lived a tech geek, chanting Web speak..."

The dot-com era of the 1990s has been called San Francisco's second Gold Rush. In place of cradles, rockers, and Long Toms, these modern Argonauts plied the mouse, the screen, and the new Ethernet, exploring the Web to strike big stock options. Like their predecessors seven score before, they were young and brash and willing to work long hours, albeit in funky warehouses south of Market near latte and sushi stands, not in filthy, freezing mining towns. However, this new generation of well educated, tech-savvy gold seekers lusted not only for success and profit; they believed they were clicking a trail to the future. And Louis Rossetto, a 40-something entrepreneur with a master's in business from Columbia, a Libertarian background, and a ponytail, was a major trailblazers. As was his wife, 30-something Jane Metcalfe, with her strong business and development background.

Jane Metcalfe and Louis Rossetto

In 1991, Rossetto and Metcalfe were jobless newcomers to the city. They were broke but they had a vision. The couple co-founded Wired Ventures, with the first goal of creating *Wired*, a monthly magazine. "We were trying to raise awareness of how the world was going to change because of technology," Metcalfe has stated. They rented vacated warehouses and set up spartan bullpen offices that turned doors into desktops and would soon be crammed with employees.

With $30K as seed money, Rossetto and Metcalfe launched *Wired* in January 1993. Taking inspiration from media mastermind Marshall McLuhan and techno-utopian Stewart Brand, *Wired* offered an incisive view of the Internet, its potential, and how its manic growth was playing out socially, economically, and politically. In his introductory editor's letter, Rossetto laid out the mag's focus: "There are a lot of magazines about technology. *Wired* is not one of them. *Wired* is about the most powerful people on the planet today: the Digital Generation."

"It's trite to say that *Wired* is talking about the convergence of media, computers, and communications," said Metcalfe at the time. "What we are really talking about is a fundamental shift in society that is being led by technology but is infiltrating every aspect of society."

Right from the start—although it didn't turn a profit until summer 1997—*Wired* was welcomed as the oracle for the Internet. Just as *Rolling Stone* divined the rock world, *Wired* forecasted the digital front. In its first issue, Rossetto declared, "the Digital Revolution is whipping through our lives like a Bengali typhoon." With its insider stories, award-winning design, and hip, frontier feel, *Wired* captivated computer geeks, venture capitalists, and graphic artists. They considered it the coolest of the digital 'zines and snapped it up, displaying it in their workspaces to buttress their own hipness. *Wired* attracted 400,000 subscribers, reflecting their lifestyle and mindset, as well as scoping out the new digital landscape.

Deriding idealism as naiveté, Rossetto habitually discussed his vision and views of *Wired* and the Internet, thrashing things out with his fellow digeratis from interns to managers to marketers. He declared: "Today is like 1948, and a new medium has reached critical mass. We're trying to help define the future of that medium before it ends up like television."

It was time to go digital. On October 27, 1994, Rossetto, Metcalfe, and company unleashed *HotWired*, the first commercial Web magazine. "This medium is not magazines with buttons, any more than television was radio with pictures," Rossetto explained. "It's Way New Journalism. It's Rational Geographic—live, twitching, the real-time nervous system of the planet."

With original content and banner ads, *HotWired* debuted *HotStats*, a real-time Web analytic tool that incorporated elementary data mining. It was the first magazine to post authors' email addresses to their articles. *HotWired* also spawned many other projects and sites, some short-lived, like *Cocktail*, *Brain Tennis*, and *Geek of the Week*, and others longer-lasting, such as *Ask Dr. Weil*, *HotBot*, and *Webmonkey*. Two staffers posted *Suck*, the first blog, which took a "no holds barred" look at Web and media issues. Wired Ventures branched into books with HardWired and television with Wired TV. In 1996, as employees put in mondo hours at their monitors, and the number of Wired Ventures' products zoomed, its headquarters became an epicenter of the digital innovation. And the first Webby Awards, designed to recognize the best websites, took place at Bimbo's 365 nightclub in North Beach.

As the stock market and the dot-com industry soared, so did San Francisco's real estate prices. Commercial properties skyrocketed 42 percent between 1997 and 1998. With the construction of the first high-rises in a decade, the median price of condos rose 40 percent from August 1998 to August 1999. Evictions—both legal and illegal—climbed, displacing many longtime residents, 70 percent of whom left the city. Many locals were displeased, to say the least, watching these newcomers bike, jog, park their SUVs, and swarm

Wired's first issue, 1993

Wired office at 510 Third Street

in restaurants around the city, always tethered to their cell phones. State income tax returns show that the gap between high earners and low earners increased 40 percent from 1994 to 1996.

Due to the warp-speed expansion of *HotWired*, now rebranded as *Wired Digital*, in 1996, Rossetto and Metcalfe reached for a critical infusion of cash, printing IPOs in day glo colors instead of the normal black and white. Their timing couldn't have been worse. The market took a severe header and their goal to take Wired Ventures public failed twice. Internally, there was major conflict and key people were shoved aside or moved on. Wired Ventures mirrored what was happening to hundreds of dot-com companies. Suddenly the money wasn't there.

In 1998, with the company valued at $500 million and $30 million in revenue, Rossetto and Metcalfe were forced to accept Providence Equity Partners as a partner. Later that year, Providence Equity sold Wired Ventures to Advanced Publications. Advanced Publications handed *Wired* magazine off to a subsidiary, Condé Nast Publications, and sold *Wired Digital* to Lycos. Rossetto and Metcalfe reaped a cool $30 million. "When *Wired* fell apart, it was devastating—both to me and Louis," Metcalfe recalled. "It was like being strapped to the front of a rocket. And then the rocket landed and you found yourself on an alien planet."

As *Wired* magazine and *Wired Digital* carried on in new hands (and do to this day), the couple stayed out of the limelight and the dot-com scene imploded in San Francisco and elsewhere. There were many casualties as dot-com companies merged, sold, or died and were dubbed dot-bombs, sending an estimated 129,310 IT workers onto the unemployment line. Analysts are at odds, but claim anywhere from 48 to 90 percent of dot-com businesses survived into 2004. Many companies and products were purchased, tweaked, and re-emerged with different names to greater success. To the south of San Francisco, in Silicon Valley, Apple remained a powerhouse, while Facebook and Google shot into the stratosphere.

Currently, San Francisco continues to think positively about tech companies, warming to social media corporations such as Groupon and Zynga. In 2011, despite controversy, the city gave tax breaks to Twitter to remain in SOMA. Opposition to these cozy arrangements persists as the class gulf widens, women and non-whites are often underrepresented, and social responsibility is lost in the drive for progress and profit. Meanwhile, venture capitalists are offering seed funds for early phase deals and new waves of entrepreneurs are moving in. San Francisco exists as it always has; a beacon on a bay that draws people from around the world. Seekers continue to show up, looking for gold, for freedom, for opportunity, for beauty in this vibrant motherlode of a city.

Mayor Gavin Newsom meets with Twitter CEO Evan Williams (center) and co-founder Biz Stone at Twitter headquarters in SOMA March 10, 2009

Metcalfe and Rossetto formed Força da Imaginaçao (Force of Imagination), an independent firm that invests in technology, media, and real estate. Metcalfe still advises several companies, serves on the board of One Economy (a non-profit that provides the poor with Internet technology and resources), and is helping plan a new facility for the UC Berkeley Art Museum and the Pacific Film Archive.

In 2006, Rossetto joined Bay Area-based TCHO chocolate as CEO and COO and Metcalfe became president. TCHO—where technology meets cacao—aims to make the best chocolate by using software to determine best methods and growing locations and by partnering with cacao growers in South America and Africa. "We're not interested in mediocrity," Rossetto asserts. "We want packaging that looks modern. We want a company that has values. We want to improve the standard of living for those we work with. It is my belief that you have to be obsessed. You have to invest humanity into your product."

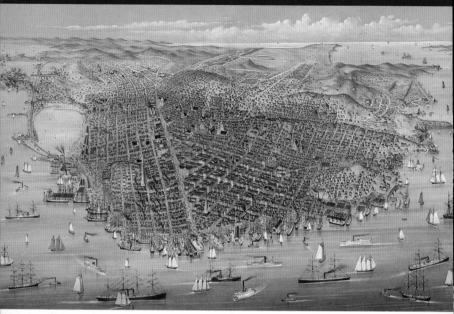

SAN FRANCISCO WALKING TOURS

   The City of San Francisco. Bird's-eye view from the bay looking southwest, c. 1878

San Francisco

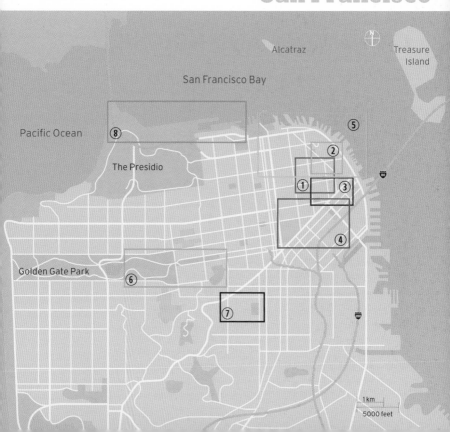

Alcatraz

Treasure Island

San Francisco Bay

Pacific Ocean

⑧

The Presidio

⑤

②

① ③

④

Golden Gate Park

⑥

⑦

1 km

5000 feet

CHINATOWN AND NOB HILL

Occupying 24 square blocks and spreading, Chinatown is home to more than 100,000 residents. It's the oldest and largest Chinese community outside of Asia and the second highest in population after New York City. Starting with the arrival of male jobseekers from Guangdong province in the 1840s, Chinese were segregated around Portsmouth Square. Since the city extended no services—sanitation, medical, roadwork, education, etc.—to Chinatown, its residents

START:
BART: Montgomery
Muni: Line 2, 3, 30, 45

END:
BART: Powell
Muni: 1, 10
Cable Car: Powell-Hyde,
Powell-Mason

TOUR TIME:
About 4 hours

CHAPTERS:
3, 9, 10, 12, 22

Chinatown Gate

Dragon-adorned streetlight

Pigtail Parade, Arnold Genthe,
c. 1900

self-governed, erecting their own hospitals, schools, churches, and theaters, and creating family and district associations for those who qualified and *tongs* (associations, some related to organized crime) for those who didn't.

When Chinatown was destroyed by the quake and fires of 1906, city officials and real estate developers wanted to relocate the Chinese to Hunter's Point and claim Chinatown's valuable land, adjacent to the Financial District. They were defeated by Chinatown residents and officials, the Chinese government, and an American-born Chinese businessman who obtained a loan from Hong Kong to rebuild Chinatown to appeal to Westerners.

The only ethnic group in U.S. history to be legally denied entrance into the country, the Chinese were also prohibited from becoming citizens, owning property, voting, and marrying non-Chinese until World War II, when FDR signed the repeal of the 1882 Chinese Exclusion Act.

1. At the intersection of Grant Avenue and Bush Street, Chinatown Gate, a.k.a. Dragon Gate, is an authentic Chinese archway. The stone pillars and jade green-tiled roof, erected in 1970, feature traditional Chinese dragon and fish sculptures and are guarded by the customary *fou* dogs.

Continue up Grant Avenue—the oldest street in San Francisco.

Notice the ornate 1920s dragon-adorned streetlights. You might also hear the *erhu*, a two-stringed Chinese violin, as you walk by tea shops, luggage shops, gift shops, and produce markets.

Turn right onto California Avenue and enter St. Mary's Square on your right.

2. To the right of the playground of St. Mary's Square is a granite and metal statue of Sun Yat-sen, first president and founding father of the Republic of China, sculpted by Benjamin Bufano.

St. Mary's Square

Statue of Sun Yat-sen

Return to California Street and turn left. Just up the street is St. Mary's Cathedral.

3. St. Mary's was built from granite quarried in China and bricks shipped around Cape Horn from New England. It was while passing St. Mary's on his way to a lecture that Emperor Norton succumbed to a stroke on the night of January 8, 1880. Inside this Paulist parish, take a brochure for a self-guided tour. A display tells the history of the church, including photos from before and after the quake.

St. Mary's Cathedral

Across the street are three buildings constructed after the quake, the Sing Chong and Sing Fat buildings, which demonstrate the post quake Chinoiserie architecture with their pagoda-like towers.

Sing Chong building

Walk back up California Street and turn right and continue up Grant Avenue to No. 631, the Far East Café.

4. Peek inside this 1920s-style restaurant with antique palace chandeliers, painted murals and carved screens imported from China more than a hundred years ago. Chinatown restaurants first introduced dim sum, chop suey, and other Chinese cuisine to Westerners.

Far East Café

Portsmouth Square, 1848

Portsmouth Square

Portsmouth Square

Portsmouth Square

Old Chinese Telephone Exchange

Continue up Grant and turn right on Clay to Portsmouth Square.

5. At Portsmouth Square on July 4, 1846, entrepreneur William Leidesdorff had the U.S. Declaration of Independence read for the first time in California. The Mexican-American War was six weeks old and San Francisco was still under Mexican rule and called Yerba Buena (good herb). On July 9, Marines from the *USS Portsmouth* rowed ashore and hoisted the stars and stripes. With the American takeover, the Mexican mayor declared martial law and Yerba Buena Plaza was re-named Portsmouth Square. Although the Treaty of Guadalupe Hidalgo formally ended the war and ceded California to the U.S. on February 2, 1848, the actions of the Portsmouth soldiers effectively ended Mexican rule in Yerba Buena and began its transition to San Francisco and American rule.

Today the square is a gathering place, often referred to as Chinatown's Living Room. In the playground is the "Tot Lot," which contains six sculptures of Chinese zodiac animals designed by Mary Fuller and commissioned by the city.

Optional: Take the pedestrian bridge across Kearny Street to the Hilton Hotel's third floor where the Chinese Culture Center mounts art shows, film festivals, and events.

Exit Portsmouth Square onto Washington Street and head left to No. 743, the Old Chinese Telephone Exchange.

6. With its pagoda and peaked roofs, the Old Chinese Telephone Exchange functions as a bank now, but was built in 1908 and employed operators who not only spoke five Chinese dialects but also knew customers' phone

numbers by heart. Before the Gold Rush, Sam Brannan set up his printing press here and published the *California Star*, the city's first newspaper and the state's second.

Buddha Bar

To see old Chinese-style bars, turn right on Grant and check out Buddha Bar at the opposite corner and Li Po on the right, a third of the way up the block.

Continue on Grant and turn left on to Jackson Street and cross the street. Turn right to enter Duncombe Alley.

Duncombe Alley

7. Exploring a few of Chinatown's forty alleys offers a glimpse into the past, as well as a view of present-day culture. The city defines an alley as a private roadway less than 32 feet wide and a block long. The tong (gang) wars mainly took place in the alleys.

All alleys have Chinese names written in Chinese characters on the street signs underneath the English name. For example, Duncombe is called Fat Boy after a 240-pound 15-year-old who lived there.

Ross Alley

Return to Jackson Street, cross back, and turn left. Turn right into Ross Alley.

8. Known as the "Street of the Gamblers," Ross Alley (Stout Alley until 1906) is Chinatown's oldest alley. It was lined with opium dens and gambling parlors, and was the setting for many a tong fight. During police raids, an alarm warned gamblers who fled via escape hatches, false floors, and trap doors. In 1964, the Beatles are rumored to have tippled at the alley's Rickshaw Bar (long closed). The alley also provided the backdrop for *Indiana Jones and the Temple of Doom*. Jun Yu at Old Yee

Ross Alley, c. 1900

Indiana Jones and the Temple of Doom

Jun Yu's Barber Shop

Old Chinatown Lane

Donaldina Cameron (center)

Door on the second floor

Chinese Free Mason Building

Barbershop has styled the hair of Frank Sinatra, Clint Eastwood, and others. A plaque with info can be found on the left and the Golden Gate Fortune Cookie Factory at No. 56, where you can watch cookies being made and try a fresh one.

Follow the alley to Washington Street and turn right. When you get to Old Chinatown Lane turn right.

9. On the left of Old Chinatown Lane, notice the Siberia Gambling Den. Aided by police, Protestant missionaries—notably Donaldina Cameron—made raids on this alley and others in Chinatown to rescue young women forced into prostitution. Brothel owners used alarms, trap doors, closets, and secret staircases to hide their enslaved workers but Cameron (who rescued more than 3,000 girls) and others were wise to their tricks. At the end of the alley on the right, look up at the second floor to spot a door that served as an escape route.

Return to Washington and cross it and enter Spofford Alley.

10. Called New Spanish Alley by the Chinese, Spofford Alley is where Nationalist Sun Yat-sen reportedly stayed when he visited. The Chinese Free Mason Building at No. 36 flies the Chinese Nationalist flag.

Return to Washington and turn right. Turn right onto Waverly Place.

11. Nicknamed the street of painted balconies for its colorful verandas, Waverly Place was also called "15¢ Street," as that's how much a haircut once cost. Many associations are located here. Look up to see the Taoist Tin How Temple at No. 127 and Norras Temple at No. 109 (the

city's oldest Buddhist Temple). The temples are located on the top floor as worshippers believe that brings them near to God. You can enter both of these and other temples. Waverly Place was also home base for Chinatown's most famous prostitute, the beautiful Ah Toy, who ran her business at No. 36. She imported girls from China, helped some gain their freedom, and lived to 99.

Waverly Place

Continue to the corner of Sacramento and view the Chinese Baptist Church and plaque. Turn right on Sacramento and walk uphill one block and turn right onto Stockton.

Tin How Temple

12. On your left at No. 827 notice the Central Chinese High School. Farther up the street at 843 Stockton is the Chinese Six Companies. A district association of merchants since the 1860s, the Chinese Six Companies, or the Consolidated Benevolent Association, protected the community against anti-Chinese violence, helping residents and interfacing with the non-Chinese community.

Chinatown brothel, c. 1900

Continue to 855 Stockton and the Kong Chow Temple on the 4th floor next to the post office.

13. Cantonese founded Kong Chow Temple in 1849. Bess Truman stopped by in 1948 during the presidential campaign. Worried her husband wouldn't be re-elected, she shook a canister of *Kau Cim* sticks until one stick tumbled out. The First Lady exchanged the stick for a slip of paper, which predicted Harry Truman would win. You can see the piece of paper at the temple.

Chinese Baptist Church

Continue up Stockton and turn left on Clay for a block uphill to No. 965 and the Chinese Historical Society Museum.

Chinese Six Companies (left) and Kong Chow Temple

Chinese Historical Society

Nob Hill from Sutter St., 1895

Nob Hill after the 1906 quake

California Street

The Mark Hopkins Hotel

14. Housed in a former YWCA building designed by Julia Morgan, the small Chinese Historical Society Museum is a fitting end for your Chinatown tour.

Nob Hill

Famous as the place where the "Big Four"–Leland Stanford, Mark Hopkins, Collis Huntington, and Charles Crocker, who monopolized the railroad industry starting in the 1860s–built their mansions in the 1870s, only to have them incinerated in the fires following the 1906 quake, Nob Hill offers magnificent views, beautiful buildings, a park, and a cathedral. The cable cars, which initially made the hill accessible for building, still run on California and Powell streets.

Continue uphill on Clay and turn left on Powell. Go two blocks and make a right on California Street. You will see the University Club (a private club and hotel) and a cable car stop at the corner. Continue past the Stanford Court Hotel (on the site of the Stanford mansion) to 999 California Street: The Mark Hopkins Hotel.

15. The Mark Hopkins Hotel is a landmark known for its history, views, luxury, and top floor. Erected in 1926 on the site of the Hopkins mansion in French Château and Spanish Renaissance styles, the hotel received its crowning glory in 1939 when owner George Smith turned its 11-room penthouse on the top (19th) floor into the famous Top of the Mark cocktail lounge. Ride the elevator up for a 360-degree view of the city and bay.

During WWII, Smith treated servicemen departing for war to a free drink. The northwest corner of the lounge was dubbed "Weepers' Corner" for the women who watched their men sail out of the Golden Gate to the Pacific Theater. The tradition continues today as soldiers buy a bottle and leave it with the bartender for other military personnel to enjoy. Whoever finishes the bottle buys the next one. The hostess has a book of soldiers' comments and photos of soldiers with their girlfriends.

Mark Hopkins' mansion, 1890s

If it's not closed off, visit the "Room of The Dons" off the lobby on the ground floor to see its historical panels. One depicts the fierce Queen Califia (California's namesake) and her posse of women in front of a gold-leaf sky.

Top of the Mark, c. 1930

Cross California to see the Fairmont Hotel. The main entrance is around the corner at 950 Mason Street.

View from "Weepers' Corner"

16. Construction of the Fairmont was almost complete when the 1906 quake struck. The hotel was gutted by the fires but survived and was renovated by Julia Morgan, who employed reinforced concrete to guard against future quakes. It was named posthumously after James Fair—one of the four "Bonanza Kings" who made their fortunes from silver—by his two daughters. Displays off the lobby tell the Fairmont's story and show artifacts. Don't miss the hotel's famed Tonga Room. In the Venetian Room in 1961 Tony Bennett first crooned what he thought would be a local song: "I Left My Heart in San Francisco." An exhibit holds memorabilia from his many return performances.

Queen Califia, "Room of The Dons"

17. Across the street at 1000 Mason is the multi-storied Brocklebank Apartment

The Fairmont

Tonga Room

Brocklebank Apartment

Herb Caen

Pacific Union Club

Huntington Park

building. In Hitchcock's 1958 thriller *Vertigo*, Scottie Ferguson (Jimmy Stewart) drives by the Pacific Union Club on his way to call on Madeleine Elster (Kim Novak), who resides at the Brocklebank Apartments (then pink). In his later years Herb Caen lived in one of these multi-million-dollar apartments. The building has put in appearances in other flicks including Gene Wilder's *The Woman in Red* and the TV series *Tales of the City*, based on Armistead Maupin's novels.

Retrace your steps on Mason and make a right on California Street. The pink Beaux Arts apartment building across the street was built in 1914. Continue on California to No. 1000—the Pacific Union Club.

18. James Flood, another of the Bonanza Kings, built this mansion in 1886. His house withstood the quake because Flood had the foresight to use brownstone, but the interior was destroyed by the fire. Flood fled and the Pacific Union Club—a conservative club of 850 well-heeled men—bought it, and has been in residence ever since.

Continue on California to Huntington Park.

19. Huntington Park, covering the site of Collis Huntington's mansion, is a good place for a rest and city views.

Cross the street to Grace Cathedral at 1100 California Street. Look back for a view of the Mark Hopkins Hotel.

20. Grace Cathedral—the third largest U.S. Episcopalian cathedral—is crafted in French Gothic style and covers the site of Crocker's mansion. Construction began in 1928 and was

completed in 1964 under the controversial Bishop James Pike. A chain-smoking alcoholic who challenged the church's conservative views, Pike ordained a woman and welcomed gays and lesbians, and was eventually forced to resign in 1966.

Grace Cathedral

The cathedral's gigantic bronze entry doors replicate Lorenzo Ghiberti's *Gates of Paradise* from the Duomo in Florence, Italy. Just inside the cathedral lies a limestone and marble labyrinth modeled after the one at Chartres. (Start at the outside, walk to the center, and return to the outside). There is also another labyrinth outside.

Bishop James Pike

The cathedral's stained-glass windows show more than 1,100 figures: in addition to saints, Pike installed contemporary figures: Jane Addams, Albert Einstein, Martin Luther King, Jr., Robert Frost, John Glenn, and Thurgood Marshall.

Stained-glass windows

Also view the faux-tile murals, a forty-four-bell English bronze carillon, and three organs (the largest has 7,466 pipes). The AIDS chapel displays an altarpiece by Keith Haring and a section of the NAMES Project's AIDS quilt.

Cross California Street to the Masonic Auditorium.

Altarpiece by Keith Haring

21. Owned by Freemasons (who arrived during the 1849 Gold Rush), the Masonic Auditorium, managed by Live Nation, has functioned as a 3,500-seat concert venue since its dedication in 1958. Statues of the four branches of the Armed Services stand outside. Inside is a frieze depicting the battle of good and evil. The mosaic window contains soil from each of California's fifty-eight counties and presents

Masonic Auditorium

Mosaic window

Cable Car Museum

Powell Street cable car

various professions along with nature scenes.

Retrace your steps on California and turn left onto Taylor Street then right onto Clay. At Mason turn left and walk one block to the Cable Car Museum. Admission to the museum is free.

Note: This .3-mile walk is less steep than others and provides interesting local color. Also, you get a good view of the Transamerica Pyramid.

22. At the Cable Car Museum you can see and hear the cables moving on huge wheels and learn about the history and workings of the iconic cars.

Optional: Take the Powell Street cable car to Market Street and watch the gripper turn around the cable car.

Jimmy Stewart and Kim Novak in *Vertigo*, 1958

NORTH BEACH

This one-square-mile neighborhood was originally a beach on the bay that greeted immigrants from Europe, South America, and Australia's penal colonies. North Beach was landfilled in the late 1800s, when Italians arrived adding "Little Italy" ambience that still exists today. The 1950s welcomed the Beats, and many of their hangouts can still be visited. The 1960s brought topless bars;

1 Old Transamerica Corporation Flatiron Building and Alioto Law Office
2 Columbus Tower
3 Tosca Café
4 Specs' Twelve Adler Museum Café
5 Vesuvio Café
6 Jack Kerouac Alley
7 City Lights Bookstore
8 Jazz mural
9 Condor Club
10 Beat Museum

11 Caffe Trieste
12 Saint Francis of Assisi Church
13 Green Street Mortuary and Club Fugazi
14 Washington Square Park: Powell, Filbert, and Union streets

Optional but well worth the few blocks of uphill walking
15 Coit Tower on Telegraph Hill
16 Telegraph Hill neighborhood and Filbert Steps

START:
BART: Embarcadero
Muni: Line 10, 41

END:
BART: Embarcadero
/ Montgomery.
Muni: Line 8X, 30, 39

Tour Time:
About 3 hours

Chapters:
2, 15, 23

Transamerica Pyramid

Old Transamerica building

Alioto Law Office

a few still remain. Now the area is home to young professionals and Chinese (from neighboring Chinatown, which continues to spread north). North Beach also has active nightlife due to its eateries and bars.

Come prepared to eat as North Beach offers an array of coffee shops, cafés, *ristorantes*, and gelato shops.

1. Start at the intersection of Columbus Avenue at Washington Street just north of the Transamerica Pyramid.

a) On the east side of Columbus, notice the Old Transamerica Corporation building with its Beaux Arts style and flatiron shape. Built in 1909 with a top floor added in 1916, it housed Banca Popolare Italiana Operaia Fugazi until John Fugazi merged his bank with A.P. Giannini's Bank of Italy in 1928, rebranded in 1930 as Bank of America. It now houses the Church of Scientology.

b) On the corner of Montgomery, note the Alioto Law Office of former mayor Joseph Alioto (in office 1968–1976) and his daughter Angela, a former supervisor. His father, a Sicilian immigrant and owner of fish canneries, met his mother on a fishing boat fleeing the 1906 quake.

Proceed north (away from the Transamerica building) on Columbus until Kearny bisects it from the left (not quite two blocks).

2. Look across the street to 916 Kearny at

a second flatiron building, verdigris with age, known as the Sentinel Building or Columbus Tower. Mayor Abe Ruef, who served time at San Quentin for graft, oversaw its re-construction following the 1906 quake and had his headquarters on the top floor. It housed Caesar's, a restaurant that was shut down for Prohibition violations and reportedly originated the Caesar salad. In the 1960s the Kingston Trio had a recording studio there, and in the 1970s Francis Ford Coppola installed his Zoetrope Studios. Café Zoetrope is on the ground floor. Cross the street to see the movie posters in the café, then recross to the same spot to continue.

Columbus Tower

Café Zoetrope

Walk to 242 Columbus, the Tosca Café, on your right.

3. The city's third-oldest bar, the Tosca Café, was recently reopened thanks to Sean Penn, a frequent patron.

Tosca Café

A few steps take you to 12 Saroyan Alley (a.k.a. Adler Alley).

4. Specs' Twelve Adler Museum Café, a dusky dive that exudes an exotic vibe due to its relic-strewn décor, fills with young and old hipsters at night.

Specs' Twelve Adler Museum Café

Cross the street to 255 Columbus: Vesuvio Café.

5. "A bohemian meeting place for artists to come to life"—that was Henri Lenoir's wish when he opened Vesuvio Café in 1948. Vesuvio was a watering hole for Jack Kerouac and other Beats. Note its pressed-tin exterior and the poem on the wall outside. Inside, Vesuvio's two floors retain a Beat ambience with 1950s photos, articles, and paintings. You can order

Vesuvio Café

Vesuvio Café

Jack Kerouac Alley

City Lights Bookstore

Dylan and Ginsberg at City Lights

Jazz mural

a drink but it's BYOF (Bring Your Own Food). Molinari's Deli is a good place to visit first. (See Detour under #12).

6. Jack Kerouac (Adler) Alley runs between Vesuvio and City Lights bookstore. Walk down this short pedestrian-only alley and see poetry and quotes gilded into the pavement and a mural as it leads, Oz-like, from Columbus Avenue and the time of the Beats to today's Chinatown and its main thoroughfare—the oldest street in the city—Grant Avenue.

7. Next door (on the North Beach side of the alley) is City Lights bookstore. Browse in Lawrence Ferlinghetti's famous shop, which remains true to its roots in the stock it carries. Check out the poetry section upstairs and the basement where Bob Dylan and many others hung out. On the bookstore's window, read about Ferlinghetti's proposed Poet's Plaza.

Continue on Columbus to North Beach's most famous intersection—Columbus and Broadway.

8. On the building diagonally across the street, notice the huge Jazz mural created by Bill Weber and Tony Klaas. Dominated by Benny Goodman, it also depicts locals including Herb Caen, Emperor Norton, and Italian fishermen.

Turn right on to Broadway.

9. At the Condor Club in 1964, Carol Doda descended on a grand piano lowered from the ceiling while singing and dancing topless. (In the 1980s, the piano ascended accidentally when a bouncer and his partner were making love on it off hours. He died, she survived.) Doda was the first to perform topless, then later, bottomless, and was the first to have

silicone injections—1,500 in total—to enlarge her breasts. The scandalous club, along with "DD" Doda, beat a few court raps and drew visitors from around the world. She now runs Carol Doda's Champagne and Lace Lingerie Boutique, and the Condor carries on, as do other strip clubs in the area.

Condor Club

10. A few steps farther is a store that holds Beat paraphernalia—T-shirts, buttons, first editions—and the Beat Museum. The museum charges $5 (with a money-back guarantee) to study the cars, records, books, shirts, photos, and paintings of the period and to learn about the Cold War and conformist context that created the crucible for the Beats.

Carol Doda

Retrace your steps on Broadway and turn right (north) on Columbus. At 308 Columbus (and elsewhere) you will notice a Barbary Coast trail medallion embedded in the pavement. To learn about the Barbary Coast area, which contained part of North Beach and other historic areas and was home to murderers, gamblers, prostitutes, drinkers, and opium smokers, go to www.barbarycoasttrail.org, which provides audio and print guides for the 3.8-mile trail.

Columbus and Broadway

Continue north on Columbus and turn right on Grant Avenue. Turn left on Vallejo and proceed to Caffe Trieste on the corner.

Beat Museum

11. Another place where the Beats met, and where Francis Ford Coppola penned the script for *The Godfather*, Caffe Trieste opened in 1956. Purportedly the first place to serve espresso on the West Coast, Caffe Trieste also introduced flavored syrups to coffee drinks. Photos of celebs decorate the walls. Starting in 1984, the owners opened a series of Caffe Triestes around the Bay Area.

Barbary Coast trail medallion

Caffe Trieste

Saint Francis of Assisi

Molinari's

Green Street Mortuary Band

Club Fugazi

12. Across Vallejo, farther up the street, you'll spot Saint Francis of Assisi, San Francisco's second-oldest Catholic church and a historic landmark with 11 murals. Built in 1849 and rebuilt after the 1906 quake, it is no longer an active parish but functions as a shrine to St. Francis. It boasts a Schoenstein organ with 1,301 pipes that you can hear during free, weekly Sunday concerts.

Continue on Vallejo to Columbus Avenue. Turn right to Green Street, then make a left.

Detour: To visit Molinari's, an old-fashioned Italian deli established in 1896, turn left and walk to nearby 373 Columbus. To rejoin the tour, retrace your steps up Columbus and continue to Green Street and turn left.

13. Green Street Mortuary at 649 Green Street (on your left) is known for the marching band it provides for funeral corteges through Chinatown.

At 678 Green Street (on your right) is Club Fugazi, a small theater and nightclub. Used by the Beats for poetry readings, it is now famous for what it claims is the longest-running musical revue in theater history. Debuting in 1974, *Beach Blanket Babylon* is an ever-changing, invariably sold out, comic send-up of current cultural characters with song, dance, and zany hairstyles and hats, culminating in a giant Golden Gate bridge headpiece. In its honor, this block of Green Street has been renamed Beach Blanket Babylon Boulevard.

Retrace your steps on Green Street and turn left onto Columbus Avenue. Walk a block to Union Street and Washington Square Park.

14. "Washington Square, which isn't square, is the heart of North Beach, which isn't a beach, and has a statue of Benjamin Franklin, not Washington."
—Kevin Wallace, writer

The park, which dates from 1850, gave refuge to people rendered homeless by the 1906 quake and fires, and was a famously photographed stopover for Joe DiMaggio and Marilyn Monroe after they got married at City Hall in 1954.

Things to see:

- The Benjamin Franklin statue with its time capsule from 1979 (for opening in 2079) in the middle of the park. Erected in 1897 by a teetotaler, it originally spouted water from Vichy, France, and other places, aspiring to deter alcohol drinkers.

- Juana Briones memorial plaque on a cement bench in the northeast corner. Her adobe house was at the opposite corner at Powell and Filbert.

- Statue of volunteer firefighters erected by a bequest of Lillie Coit on the park's west side.

- Saints Peter and Paul Church: This hulk of neo-Gothic architecture is overseen by the Salesians and contains a 40-foot altar of Italian marble with Leonardo da Vinci's *Last Supper* carved into it. In 1919 Father Oreste Trincheri founded the Salesian Boys Club to mitigate juvenile delinquency and teach boys, including the DiMaggio brothers, sports. Saints Peter and Paul served the Italian community for decades and witnessed Joe DiMaggio's marriage to his first wife in 1941.

Washington Square Park

Columbus Ave. to the park, 1906

Statue of Benjamin Franklin

Saints Peter and Paul Church

Washington Square, Filbert Street and Telegraph Hill 1866–67

243

Filbert Street and Coit Tower

View from Coit Tower

WPA mural

Filbert Steps

1360 Montgomery in *Dark Passage*, 1947

You can end your tour here, or enjoy the shops and restaurants on Powell, Filbert, and Union streets.

Consider taking a 12-minute (.4 mile) walk uphill to Coit Tower on Telegraph Hill. Start by going east on Union. Turn left on Kearny, then right on Filbert. Alternatively, take Muni bus No. 39.

15. Coit Tower and Pioneer Park atop Telegraph Hill (earlier known as Goat Hill due the herds that once roamed there) offer views of the city, especially of the Embarcadero, Treasure Island, and the Bay Bridge. Learn about Coit Tower, erected in 1929, and its benefactor, the free-living Lillie Hitchcock Coit. There's also a statue of Columbus, arms outspread and looking out at the bay. Go inside the tower to see WPA murals that vividly illustrate the Depression era in the Bay Area.

16. To explore the surrounding neighborhood with its lovely houses, gardens, art, and wild green parrots, exit the tower area to the southeast and take the Filbert steps down to Montgomery. Notice 1360 Montgomery, an Art Deco apartment building inscribed with a sea theme. It served as Bogart and Bacall's hideout in the film *Dark Passage*. Turn right until you reach Alta. Turn left to 60 Alta to see *Tales of the City* writer Armistead Maupin's former apartment along with other interesting houses, and a view at the end of the street. Turn right on Alta and/or go to the end of Montgomery for more beautiful houses and vistas.

Return to Montgomery and turn left. Turn right and take Union back towards Columbus.

Lauren Bacall and Humphrey Bogart in *Dark Passage*, 1947

UNION SQUARE AND FINANCIAL DISTRICT

Union Square Park, ringed by hotels, art galleries, and stores, and adjacent to the Financial District, dates back to 1839. When gold-seekers rushed in, they camped on it. As the land was developed, temples and churches sprouted up around it, including a Unitarian Society. Its minister, Thomas Starr King, led pro-Union rallies

UNION SQUARE
1. St. Francis Hotel
2. Union Square Park
3. Neiman Marcus rotunda interior
4. Maiden Lane
5. Gump's

FINANCIAL DISTRICT
6. The White House (255 Sutter)
7. Hallidie Building (130 Sutter)
8. 111 Sutter
9. Mill's Building (220 Montgomery)
10. The Russ Building (235 Montgomery)
11. 300 Montgomery

12. Merchants Exchange Building (465 California)
13. 400 California
14. 555 California
15. 580 California
16. 420 Montgomery
17. 505 Montgomery
18. 605 Commercial
19. 608 Commercial
20. 624 Commercial
21. 550 Montgomery
21. Transamerica Pyramid

START:
BART: Powell
Muni: Line 2, 38

END:
BART: Embarcadero
Muni: Line 1, 10, 41

Tour Time:
About 4 hours

Chapters:
3, 4, 7, 10, 15

there during the Civil War, which is how it got its name. After the 1906 quake, the square was home to campers again, and when temporary buildings went up, it was nicknamed the "Little St. Francis."

1. On the southwest corner of Union Square sits the St. Francis Hotel, built because trustees for railroad baron Charles Crocker's estate thought it would be a solid investment for his children. The trustees went on a world tour of top hotels and invested $2.5 million in two 12-story towers. The St. Francis opened in 1904, and was one of few buildings on the square to withstand the big quake two years later. Though gutted by the post-quake fires, the hotel was restored and more wings and a 32-story tower were added. Step into the lobby to see photos of yesteryear plus the 10-foot Viennese clock.

St. Francis Hotel

In 1975 President Gerald Ford was exiting the hotel to Post Street after giving a luncheon speech when Sara Jane Moore fired her revolver at him. An ex-Marine jostled her arm so the bullet hit a wall. Ford was fine and Moore was sentenced to life in prison.

Ford assassination attempt, 1975

Cross Powell Street to enter Union Square Park.

2. The multi-leveled park holds historic yew trees, an outdoor café, and free Wi-Fi. Each corner displays a heart sculpture that is auctioned off annually to benefit the San Francisco General Hospital Foundation. Emperor Norton decreed that the park raise a Christmas tree each year. The tradition now includes a menorah and an ice rink.

Union Square Park

A monument at the center honors Admiral George Dewey for his role in the Spanish-American War and President William McKinley, who was present for the monument's groundbreaking and assassinated a few months later. His successor, President Theodore Roosevelt, dedicated the monument in 1903.

Heart sculpture at the square

Exit the park at the southeast corner and cross to Neiman Marcus.

Admiral Dewey Monument

3. As you enter Neiman Marcus look up at the rotunda dome and its stained glass with a ship in its oval center. A plaque on the wall to your right describes the stained glass and its history. Felix Verdier sailed into the bay in 1850 on a ship called *City of Paris* bearing fine French goods. Flush gold miners rowed out to the ship and bought the lot before Verdier's ship docked, many paying with gold dust. In 1896 the Verdiers erected the City of Paris department store, rebuilding it after the 1906 quake. It sat at this site until 1981 when its new owner—Neiman Marcus—demolished the revered Beaux Arts building despite its landmark designation. The City of Paris's Latin motto *"Fluctuat nec mergitur"*, inscribed in the stained glass's uppermost panel, speaks to its survival: "It floats but doesn't sink."

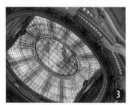
The City of Paris stained glass

Re-opened City of Paris, 1909

Exit the store and walk straight ahead (north) on Stockton, paralleling Union Square Park. Turn right onto Maiden Lane.

4. Nearby the churches bordering Union Square was Morton Street, renamed Maiden Lane in 1922. Beginning in the 1800s, Morton Street was the center of the red-light district and notorious for having the cheapest, basest "cow-yards" (brothels) with hundreds of rooms per floor. The police provided security and took

Maiden Lane

Barbary Coast ladies, 1890

Xanadu Gallery

Interior of the gallery

Gump's at 135 Post Street

Ch'ing Dynasty Buddha

their cut and the prostitutes, who were kept under lock and key, could refuse no customer and died early. The 1906 quake wiped the slate clean and the eventual result is today's pleasant, upscale lane.

Walk to 140 Maiden Lane—the mustard-bricked Xanadu Gallery. Built in 1949, it's the only Frank Lloyd Wright building in the city and was originally designed for the V.C. Morris Gift Shop. The bright red tile embedded in a square of cement to the left of the door is Wright's personal marker. Go inside to see the spiral ramp—the prototype for the one Wright designed for the Guggenheim Museum in Manhattan. Walk up the ramp and enjoy its glass inserts that resemble escaping water bubbles.

Continue down Maiden Lane and turn left on Grant Avenue then right on Post Street to 135 Post: Gump's.

5. Created by two Gump brothers with their Gold Rush millions in 1861, Gump's is renowned for its Asian artifacts collection. Step inside to see the 19th-century Ch'ing Dynasty gilded wood Buddha.

To cross into the Financial District, start by retracing your steps on Post Street.

Financial District: An Architectural Tour

When the cast-iron buildings melted in the 1906 earthquake, the city rebuilt using steel and added floors. For years, the city's tallest buildings have been clustered in "FiDi," the Financial District.

Starting in the 1980s, due to new earthquake-proof building techniques and the lifting of height restrictions, a building boom began. It was countered by a "skyscraper revolt" by those, including Herb Caen, who opposed what they deemed the Manhattanization of the city.

FiDi is home to banks, corporate headquarters, and other businesses. It also houses consulates, as does the affluent Pacific Heights district to the west overlooking the bay. This tour allows you to see banks and other buildings from different architectural eras and winds up at the city's tallest edifice: the Transamerica Pyramid.

Financial District

301-303 Sutter Street

From Post Street turn right on Stockton and right again on Sutter.

Sutter Street

As you proceed down Sutter, notice 301–303 Sutter, which typifies smaller 19th-century buildings.

6. 255 Sutter: The White House, an illustrious French-accented department store with a white façade (hence its name) by Albert Pissis, who also was the architect for the Flood mansion on Nob Hill. The building illustrates the tripartite Beaux Arts style with its arch over the door on the first floor, windows on the second floor, and cornice roof.

7. 130 Sutter: Considered the first U.S. building to use a glass wall, it was named after cable-car inventor Andrew Hallidie and was designed by Willis Polk. The 1918 Hallidie building sealed Polk's reputation as a pioneer architect.

255 Sutter Street

130 Sutter Street

Willis Polk

111 Sutter Street

220 Montgomery Street

235 Montgomery Street

300 Montgomery Street

California Street, west from
Sansome Street, c. 1860-1906

8. 111 Sutter: This historic 22-story, terra-cotta clad, steel-frame French Romanesque building was completed in 1927. According to Dashiell Hammett experts, noir detective Sam Spade had his office here. Walk through the vaulted lobby with its colorful, ribbed ceiling and turn right. Wall hangings reveal the history of the building, including Spade's tenancy.

Continue on Sutter and turn left on Montgomery Street, sometimes referred to as the "Wall Street of the West."

Montgomery Street Part 1

9. 220 Montgomery: Known as the Mills Building, 220 Montgomery was designed by Chicago architects Burnham and Root and completed in 1891. The staircase in the lobby retains the original Jaune Fleuri marble, complimented by black Belgian marble and Roman travertine, with an inlaid marble floor pattern added during a 1988 remodeling.

10. 235 Montgomery: The Russ Building, a Neo-Gothic skyscraper completed in 1927, reigned as the city's tallest building until 1964. Named for Emanuel Russ, who bought the site for $75 in the 1840s, the building was the first in the city to have an indoor parking garage.

11. 300 Montgomery: Erected in 1917 as the world headquarters of the Bank of America, the building's Neo-Gothic style is evident in the curtain wall of brick and concrete exterior as well as in its lobby. In 1969 the bank moved its headquarters. Pick up the story at 555 California Street below.

Continue on Montgomery Street and turn right on California Street

California Street

12. 465 California: The Merchants Exchange
Building skyscraper was designed by Daniel
Burnham and Willis Polk in the Beaux Arts
style and completed in 1903. Go inside to view
the barrel-vaulted lobby, composed of marble,
gold leaf, and bronze, and designed by Julia
Morgan. The Julia Morgan Ballroom on the
15th floor has welcomed presidents from Teddy
Roosevelt to Barack Obama.

465 California Street

Julia Morgan

13. 400 California: In the basement of the main
branch of the Bank of California you'll find the
Museum of Money, showcasing old coins and
currencies. You can learn about the Vigilante
Committees of the 1850s and see the pistol
used in the fatal Terry-Broderick duel.

Retrace your steps on California, cross
Montgomery, and continue on California.

400 California Street

14. 555 California: This is the "New Bank
of America" building where the company
headquartered from 1969 until relocating to
Charlotte, North Carolina, in 1998. The roof was
featured in *Dirty Harry* and the plaza in *The
Towering Inferno*.

555 California Street

15. 580 California: Completed in 1987, this
postmodern 23-story tower is referred to as
the Grim Reaper building. On each side of its
mansard roof are three white, hollow statues—
twelve in all, each 12 feet tall. They are maidens
without faces or hands shrouded in classical,
flowing gowns. Sculptor Muriel Castanis titled
her work *The Corporate Goddesses* and was
inspired by women's relationship to fabrics.

580 California

Retrace your steps back to Montgomery and
turn left.

420 Montgomery Street

505 Montgomery Street

Hudson's Bay Company plaque

608 Commercial Street

Ambling along Montgomery Street showing Bummer & Lazarus, Emperor Norton I. and Frederick Coombs, Edward Jump, c. 1861

Montgomery Street Part 2

16. 420 Montgomery: The free Wells Fargo History Museum explores Gold Rush history and features a stagecoach you can sit in on the second floor. Also exhibited are Emperor Norton's bank notes, artifacts from the 1906 conflagration, as well as souvenirs from the 1894 Midwinter Expo in Golden Gate Park and the 1915 Panama–Pacific International Expo.

17. 505 Montgomery: This "Hypodermic Needle Building," as it's been labeled, is a chameleon: Its base is Art Deco but as it spires up 24 stories, it morphs to a modern, mansard shape. The "needle" replicates the one on the Empire State Building.

Continue on Montgomery and turn left on to Commercial Street.

Commercial Street

18. 605 Commercial: During the 1840s, when the city was called Yerba Buena and ruled by Spain, this building was on the waterfront and housed the Hudson's Bay Company, which shipped animal furs and pelts east.

19. 608 Commercial: On the opposite side of street, starting in 1854, stood the first U.S. Branch Mint in California. The brick front remains with added stories, though the Mint moved across town in 1875. Today it is inhabited by the Bank of Canton and the free Pacific Heritage Museum. The museum details the Mint's history with photos, blueprints, coins, and other relics.

20. Farther down the street, at 624 Commercial, there once was a boarding house with a room

that served as the palace for Emperor Norton, a beloved eccentric who sauntered the streets from the 1850s until his death in 1880.

Return to Montgomery and turn left and continue on Montgomery.

Montgomery Street Part 3

21. 550 Montgomery: Built in 1908, this Beaux Arts building was the first headquarters of A.P. Giannini's Bank of Italy (renamed Bank of America in 1931). He positioned his desk in the lobby to encourage customers to approach him. Notice the Bank of Italy initials on the brass teller cages and the ornate ceiling.

22. 600 Montgomery: Completed in 1972 and coated in crushed quartz, the Transamerica Pyramid rises forty-eight stories to a glass pyramid cap that encapsulates an aircraft warning beacon and seasonal white light. Enter the lobby to see a virtual view from the top via four cameras pointing in the four cardinal directions. Additionally, a plaque tells the story of the 1856 shooting death of newspaper editor James King of William.

The Transamerica Pyramid site is also where A.P. Giannini set up his plank-and-chair bank and began making loans following the 1906 temblor. In 1928 he established a holding company, Transamerica Corp., which no longer owns or occupies the iconic building bearing its name. The building occupies the site where the Niantic Hotel inn and bar operated when the *Niantic*, formerly a whaling ship, was dragged ashore after being abandoned by its crew for the gold fields in 1849.

550 Montgomery Street

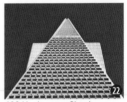
600 Montgomery Street

A. P. Giannini

The Niantic Hotel in 1850

Transamerica Pyramid

CIVIC CENTER AND MARKET STREET

This tour takes you to many government institutions, museums, and public buildings, providing a rich civic, historic, and modern look at San Francisco.

1. United Nations Plaza
2. Asian Art Museum
3. Public Library
4. City Hall
5. Davies Symphony Hall
6. War Memorial Opera House
7. Veteran's Building
8. British Motor Car Distributors
9. Olive Street Murals
10. Old U.S. Mint

11. St. Patrick's Catholic Church
12. Contemporary Jewish Museum
13. Yerba Buena Gardens
14. SFMOMA (re-opens early 2016)
15. Museum of the African Diaspora
16. California Historical Society
17. Cartoon Art Museum
18. Lotta's Fountain
19. Wells Fargo Bank
20. Palace Hotel

START:
BART: Civic Center
/UN Plaza
Muni: Line 5, 19, 21, F, J,
K, L, M, N, T

END:
BART: Montgomery
Muni: Line 5, 10, 21, 31,
38, F, J, K, L, M, N, T

TOUR TIME:
About 4 hours

CHAPTERS:
6, 14, 28

United Nations Plaza

Pioneer Monument

Asian Art Museum

Start at United Nations Plaza.

1. Completed in 1975 in conjunction with BART, United Nations Plaza commemorates the signing of the UN Charter in 1945 in the nearby War Memorial building (see #6) and is a major transportation hub.

Go south on UN Plaza and head right, skirting the concrete sculpture on your left. Turn right onto Fulton Street. You will pass an oval plaza with a bronze sculpture—Pioneer Monument, a.k.a. James Lick monument. Installed in 1894, for years it sat on the site of the City Hall brought down by the 1906 quake. When the new library was built (see #3) the monument was relocated due to its controversial portrayal of Native Americans, mediated by the addition of a plaque delineating the history of Native Americans in San Francisco on the base.

Across the street to the north is the Asian Art Museum building. For the entrance, continue on Fulton and turn right onto Larkin Street.

2. Housed in the former library rebuilt after the 1989 quake, the Asian Art Museum boasts one of the world's most extensive Asian art collections. It also contains a great cafeteria and a gift store.

Go south on Larkin (toward Fulton) and turn left on Grove Street to No. 100: The Public Library.

3. Newly built and opened in 1996, the Public Library consists of seven floors with more than seven million books. Step inside to see its five-story atrium and exhibits. Tours are free.

Cross Larkin to Civic Center Plaza and walk
toward City Hall. On your left is the 7,000-seat
Bill Graham Civic Auditorium. One of
several Civic Center buildings built in classic
Beaux Arts style, it was designed for the 1915
Panama–Pacific International Expo. Retrofitted
after its back wall collapsed during the 1989
quake, the auditorium was renamed in 1991
after the late rock promoter.

Public Library

4. City Hall offers free tours, both self-guided
and docent led. This Beaux Arts building
opened in 1915, just in time for the Panama–
Pacific Expo. Modeled after St. Peter's Basilica
in the Vatican, its dome is the fifth largest
in the world and higher than the Capitol in
Washington, DC. In 1954, Marilyn Monroe
married Joe DiMaggio in a judge's chambers
on the third floor. In 1978, Dan White killed
Mayor George Moscone and Supervisor Harvey
Milk on the second floor. The White Night riots
that followed White's lenient sentence (7 years)
in 1979 damaged the building slightly. In 2004
Mayor Gavin Newsome granted a marriage
license to Del Martin and Phyllis Lyon, the first
same-sex couple to wed in the city; it was later
voided by the California Supreme Court. After
the legalization of same-sex marriage statewide
in 2008, Martin and Lyon were again married
by Newsome at City Hall.

Bill Graham Civic Auditorium

City Hall

Monroe-DiMaggio wedding, 1954

Exit City Hall and circle the building to the
southwest corner and the intersection of Van
Ness and Grove. Diagonally across the street
is a modern, curved building recessed from the
sidewalk: Louise M. Davies Symphony Hall.
Cross Van Ness and you're there.

White Night riots, May 21, 1979

Louise M. Davies Symphony Hall

Henry Moore bronze sculpture

War Memorial Opera House

Main hall of the Opera House

Signing of the UN Charter, 1945

5. In front of Davies Hall at the corner of Van Ness and Grove is a Henry Moore bronze sculpture. Opened in 1980 and named after its major benefactor, Davies Symphony Hall is home to San Francisco's symphony orchestra, which performs year round, usually under music director Michael Tilson Thomas.

Note: There are low-priced tours of #5–7— Davies Hall, the Opera House, and Herbst Theatre, inside the Veteran's Building—every Monday (except holidays) from 10 a.m.–2 p.m. on the hour. The tours begin at the Grove Street entrance of Davies Hall. Call 415-552-8338 for information.

Continue north on Van Ness to the Opera House.

6. Built in 1932 to honor WWI soldiers, the War Memorial Opera House was the last Beaux-Arts style building to be built at the Civic Center. Part of the San Francisco War Memorial and Performing Arts Center, it has been home to the San Francisco Opera since opening night in 1932; it also hosts the San Francisco Ballet. Go inside to see the grand interior with its barrel-vaulted and coffered ceiling. The main hall has an enormous aluminum and glass chandelier. After suffering damage from the 1989 quake, the building was repaired and seismically enhanced.

Continue north on Van Ness to the Veteran's Building.

7. A twin to the War Memorial Opera House, the Veteran's Building was built in the same

year (1932) by the same architect (Arthur Brown, Jr., who worked with G. Albert Lansburgh on the Opera House) to also honor WWI soldiers. On June 26, 1945, after a two-month conference at the Opera House, representatives from 50 nations signed the UN Charter on the stage of the Herbst Theatre. Eight Beaux Arts murals created for the 1915 Panama–Pacific Expo decorate the walls of the theater—now a concert hall—and five chandeliers hang from its blue and gold-leaf ceiling.

Herbst Theatre

Continue north on Van Ness. Next is the State Office Building on the corner of Van Ness and McAllister. Leave the Civic Center behind as you stay on Van Ness for .3 miles to arrive at No. 901: British Motor Car Distributors.

State Office Building

8. Here, in 1927, a Packard car dealership opened with a radio broadcast from a tower atop the building and a bevy of movie actresses. At night, colored lights simulated sunrise to moonrise in 20 minutes. Bernard Maybeck, architect of the Palace of Fine Arts, designed the showroom to be a glamorous movie stage with a backstage for storing and servicing the cars.

British Motor Car Distributors

Retrace your steps a half block to Ellis Street and cross Van Ness. Walk down Ellis Street. Turn left on Polk Street and right onto Olive.

Showroom

9. You have entered the Tenderloin, a designated historic district with a long history of vice, jazz, and gay life. The murals on Olive Street reflect the Tenderloin's recent history, which began in the '70s when Southeast Asian immigrants settled here after the Vietnam War.

Tenderloin mural

Tenderloin mural

Glide Memorial Church

The Old U.S. Mint

St. Patrick's Catholic Church

Contemporary Jewish Museum

Continue to the end of Olive Street. Turn right on Larkin. Turn left on Ellis. Cross Van Ness and continue on Ellis Street.

Optional: A short journey to Glide Memorial Church, a Methodist church of 10,000 members led for decades by Reverend Cecil Williams and his Poet Laureate wife Janice Mirikitani. The church was early to include rock musicians and features lively music to this day. It helps people with HIV and AIDS and those afflicted by substance addiction, mental health issues, and domestic violence.

To visit Glide Church, turn left on Taylor Street and go to No. 333. To rejoin the tour, retrace your steps on Taylor and continue south.

If you skipped Glide Church, from Ellis, turn right on Taylor Street. Turn left onto Eddy Street. Turn right onto Cyril Magnin Street/Fifth Street. Continue to 88 Fifth Street: the Old U.S. Mint.

10. Crafted in Greek Revival style in 1874, the Old Mint held a third of the nation's gold reserves in its ornate interior until 1937. Referred to as the "Granite Lady" due to its building material, it is on its way to becoming a museum. It currently offers monthly tours, exhibits, and events.

Continue on Fifth and turn left on Mission Street to No. 756: St. Patrick's Catholic Church.

11. St. Patrick's is a Gothic-style church dating from 1851 and the Gold Rush, with a nave layout and stained-glass windows.

Continue on Mission, entering the Yerba Buena District, to No. 736 Mission: the Contemporary Jewish Museum.

12. A modern building that first opened its doors in 1984, the Contemporary Jewish Museum hosts exhibits on topics from kibutz life to the lives and legacies of Houdini, Gertrude Stein, and Maurice Sendak.

Continue to No. 701: Yerba Buena Gardens.

13. Controversial from its conception in the 1960s and for the buildings it swept away in its urban renewal wake, Yerba Buena Gardens opened in 1981. It has many components: Yerba Buena Center for the Arts (a theater), Moscone Center (a convention and exhibit hall), Moscone Ballroom, a children's center, and Zeum (a rooftop space for collaborations between artists and youths).

The 5.5-acre esplanade features a meadow, butterfly garden, waterfalls, memorials, sculptures, and a café. A major site is the Martin Luther King, Jr. Memorial. It is composed of a waterfall, inscriptions of his words, photos of the Civil Rights movement, and poems. Another site is the Ohlone Indian memorial, which includes a sculpture, redwood trees, and a pool. On the upper terrace there are gardens and glass pyramids that reveal the Moscone Convention Center below.

Continue on Mission.

If #14, SFMOMA (San Francisco Museum of Modern Art) is open (call 415-358-7200 or check

Yerba Buena Gardens

Yerba Buena Center for the Arts

Moscone Center Ballroom

Martin Luther King, Jr. Memorial

Esplanade

SFMOMA

Museum of the African Diaspora

California Historical Society

Historical Society interior

The Cartoon Art Museum

online): Turn right on Third Street to reach SFMOMA's entrance at 151 Third Street.

If #14, SFMOMA is closed, proceed on Mission to #15, the Museum of the African Diaspora, at 685 Mission.

14. Starting in June 2013, SFMOMA closed for a major expansion and is due to reopen in early 2016. For the duration, SFMOMA asks people to "Think outside the building" and visit its exhibits and events around the Bay Area.

15. Housed in the new St. Regis Museum Tower, MoAD (Museum of the African Diaspora) opened in 2005. It traces all Homo sapiens to Africa and documents the history of slave trade in North and South America, as well as freedom struggles in Africa and other subjects via interactive and video exhibits. It also hosts film, photography, and lecture series.

Continue on Mission to No. 678: the California Historical Society.

16. The California Historical Society offers changing exhibits as well as photographs, costumes, paintings, a research library, and a bookstore. Admission is free, though a donation is suggested.

Continue on Mission to No. 655: the Cartoon Art Museum.

17. The Cartoon Art Museum displays cartoon art including Sunday funnies, Saturday morning cartoons, anime, comic books, and graphic novels. It has five galleries, a research

library, a bookstore, some 6,000 original pieces, and puts on 9 to 12 major exhibitions annually along with classes for adults and kids.

Retrace your steps on Mission to Annie Street and turn right. Turn left on Stevenson, then right on Third Street. Turn right again on Market Street.

Market and Third Street

At the corner of Market and Third are three buildings (all destroyed and rebuilt after 1906) of San Francisco's three former newspapers owned by it three pre-eminent families: *The Call* (on the northeast corner and owned by the Spreckels), *The Examiner* (on the southeast corner and owned by the Hearsts), and *The Chronicle* (on the southwest corner and owned by the de Youngs).

Call building on fire, 1906

Proceed on Market and cross to the copper-colored, cast-iron fountain—Lotta's Fountain—at the intersection of Market, Geary, and Kearny streets.

Lotta's Fountain

18. In 1875 actress Lotta Crabtree donated this fountain, modeled after a prop lighthouse used in one of her plays. Lotta's Fountain not only survived the quake of 1906, but served as a posting place for notices of the dead, missing, and found. Since then, every April 18th at 5:12 a.m. public officials, firefighters, and locals gather for a moment of silence. Afterwards a band plays "San Francisco" and speeches and libations flow.

Luisa Tetrazzini, 1911

A plaque on the fountain commemorates Christmas Eve 1910 when the town was rewarded for its post-quake rebuilding efforts

Tetrazzini in San Francisco, 1910

Wells Fargo Bank

The Palace Hotel

The Palace Hotel, 1875

Garden Court

Maxfield Parrish's *Pied Piper*
painting at the Palace Hotel bar

by the appearance of Italian opera singer
Luisa Tetrazzini.

Continue on Market Street to Montgomery
Street. The streetlamp posts were installed after
the 1906 quake to cut down on looting. At the
tri-section of Market, Montgomery, and Post is
Wells Fargo Bank (at 1 Montgomery).

19. Architect Willis Polk designed this Italian
Renaissance building at 1 Montgomery, which
has hosted a succession of banks and was
completed in 1908. Notice the white marble and
bronze lobby and the vampires in the bronze
window trim. The building has been repeatedly
remodeled, including having its upper story
lopped off in 1983. A roof garden crowns it
currently.

Turn right (south) on Montgomery and walk to
No. 2: the Palace Hotel.

20. The Palace Hotel carries so much history
and elegant architecture that the hotel and SF
City Guides (www.sfcityguides.org) provide
free tours. There's the Garden Court, the
bar with Maxfield Parrish's 1909 painting,
Pied Piper, and amusing exhibits during the
holidays that render familiar scenes in cookies,
cakes, and candies.

Market Street, toward the ferries, c. 1892

City Hall before 1906

Market Street on August 16, 1945, end of the World War II

EMBARCADERO TO GHIRARDELLI SQUARE

The Embarcadero (Spanish for wharf) stretches from AT&T Park (Giants Stadium) past the Bay Bridge to its last pier—Pier 45, neighbor to Fisherman's Wharf. The Embarcadero packs a bevy of piers, museums, amusements, and panoramic views of San Francisco Bay. Its piers are embarkation points for Alcatraz, Oakland and other East Bay towns, and Sausalito and other

❶ Rincon Park
❷ Pier 14
❸ Ferry Building
❹ Embarcadero Center/ Justin Herman Plaza
❺ Pier 7
❻ Pier 15: Exploratorium
❼ Pier 33: Alcatraz ferry and displays
❽ Pier 39
❾ Pier 45: WWII Liberty ship, submarine, and Musée Mécanique
❿ Fisherman's Wharf

⓫ Cannery
⓬ Maritime Visitor Center in the Haslett Warehouse
⓭ Hyde Street Pier
⓮ Aquatic Park Bathhouse Building/ SF National Maritime Museum
⓯ Buena Vista Café
⓰ Ghirardelli Square

California Women's Army Corps members at Fisherman's Wharf, 1951

Pier 45

Pier 43

Pier 41

Jefferson St.

Pier 35

Beach St.

North Point St.

Columbus Ave.

Francisco St.

Pier 31

TELEGRAPH
HILL

NORTH
BEACH

Pier 27-29

Coit
Tower

Pier 23

Pier 19

Leavenworth St.

Jones St.

Taylor St.

Mason St.

Washington
Square

Kearny St.

Montgomery St.

Sansome St.

Battery St.

Front St.

Pier 17

Pier 15

Hyde St.

Davis St.

Pier 9

RUSSIAN
HILL

Broadway St.

Pier 5

Pier 3

Pier 1

Chestnut St.

Lombard St.

Greenwich St.

Filbert St.

Union St.

Green St.

Vallejo St.

CHINATOWN

Portsmouth
Square

Transamerica
Pyramid

Pier 2

Pacific Ave.

Jackson St.

Washington St.

NOB
HILL

FINANCIAL
DISTRICT

Steuart St.

Clay St.

Grace
Cathedral

Main St.

Sacramento St.

Stockton St.

Grant St.

Beale St.

California St.

Powell St.

Fremont St.

1st St.

Pine St.

Bush St.

Sutter St.

Post St.

2nd St.

New Montgomery St.

Geary St.

DOWNTOWN

Union
Square

3rd St.

O'Farrell St.

TENDERLOIN

Ellis St.

Market St.

4th St.

Yerba Buena
Gardens

Eddy St.

5th St.

SOMA

Franklin St.

Van Ness St.

Polk St.

Larkin St.

Turk St.

Golden Gate Ave.

6th St.

McAllister St.

7th St.

Howard St.

Folsom St.

Harrison St.

Bryant St.

Brannan St.

Civic
Center
Plaza

8th St.

9th St.

Mission St.

ton St.

ove St.

ayes St.

Fell St.

Oak St.

10th St.

11th St.

Townsend St.

King St.

Berry St.

START:
BART: Embarcadero
Muni: Line 5, 14, 21, 31,
38, F, J, K, L, M, N, T

END:
BART: Jones St/Beach St
Muni: Line 19, 30, 47, 49
Cable Car: Powell-Hyde

TOUR TIME:
About 4 hours

CHAPTERS:
5, 18, 19, 22

Bay Bridge from Rincon Park

Cupid's Span sculpture

Information kiosk

North Bay towns via ferry, boat, or BART. Many busses and light rail cars also stop at the Embarcadero, making it a transportation hub.

The demolition of the "Dambarcadero" Freeway (Herb Caen's name for the detested, four-tiered, Bay-view-blocking Embarcadero Freeway) after the 1989 quake brought light and renovation to this derelict area. Locals and visitors can travel the bay by foot, bike, Segway or pedicab, yellow Gocar, or vintage streetcar (painted different colors according to their city—U.S. or international—of origin).

This is a continuous walk northwest (away from the Bay Bridge) on the Embarcadero unless other directions are provided. Occasionally, you will see bronze disks set in the pavement labeled "Bay Trail" with information on history and nature.

1. At Rincon Park you can sit on the wall dotted with bronze sea creatures and look out at the Bay Bridge. See where it touches Yerba Buena Island (which extends left to manmade Treasure Island, named after the Robert Louis Stevenson book). Farther along, notice the Port of Oakland, where huge cranes hoist containers on and off ships. On the city (San Francisco) side, you notice *Cupid's Span*, the 60-foot-high painted bow and arrow sculpture made out of fiberglass and stainless-steel by Claes Oldenburg and Coosje van Bruggen.

As you walk to the next stop, you pass vertical kiosks with alternating black-and-white cubes on top. The second one you pass tells about the 1934 dock strike.

2. Pier 14 reopened as a pedestrian pier in 2006. A kiosk relates the pier's history. If you stroll up Pier 14, it offers a sweeping vista of Angel Island (big, with few buildings, and the entry point for thousands of Asians), the Bay Bridge, the ferries, and, on the city side, of Telegraph Hill and Coit Tower. Pier 14 has modern spinning metal chairs—great for swiveling around to view the bay.

Strolling the Embarcadero

Note: Even-numbered piers are located southeast of the Ferry Building; odd-numbers are northwest.

Pier 14

Optional: Take a short detour to the small, free San Francisco Railway Museum and learn about the city's streetcars and walk by the Audiffred Building at 1–21 Mission Street. To do this, continue up the Embarcadero and turn left on Mission Street, then turn right on Steuart Street until the museum. Retrace your steps to continue to stop #3.

View from Pier 14

As you walk on to #3, notice the old brick building with the mansard roof. Built in 1889 in the Second Empire style by nostalgic Frenchman Hippolyte d'Audiffret, the Audiffred Building was a union hall for maritime workers. Legend holds that it survived the fires after the 1906 quake because a bartender on the ground floor "encouraged" firefighters with two quarts of whiskey apiece and a cart of wine. During the 1934 dockworkers' strike, police shot two dockworkers dead in front of the building, a tragedy that became called "Bloody Thursday" and is commemorated yearly on the spot. Blocked by the Embarcadero Freeway erected in 1955, the building fell into ruin and was further devastated by fire in 1979. Declared a national landmark in 1981 and restored, it is now a restaurant.

San Francisco Railway Museum

Audiffred Building

The Ferry Building

Bell Tower

Gandhi statue

Vaillancourt Fountain

Justin Herman Plaza

3. The Ferry Building is the port for ferries to Alameda, Marin County (Angel Island, Larkspur, Sausalito, and Tiburon), Oakland, and Vallejo. Restored in 2002, the building hosts upscale markets and cafés and a Farmer's Market on Tuesdays, Thursdays, and Saturdays. Designed in 1892 after the 12th-century Giralda bell tower in Seville, Spain, the Beaux Arts, Boston-made clock has the world's largest hand-wound mechanism—with four dials, each 22 feet in diameter—which still works even though the clock now runs electrically.

Although it is easy to miss in a parking lot behind the Ferry Building, vandals manage to find a statue of Gandhi (donated by the Gandhi Memorial International Foundation in 1988) and repeatedly remove his glasses.

Cross the street to the Embarcadero Center that encompasses Justin Herman Plaza.

4. Named after the controversial head of re-development in the 1960s, Justin Herman Plaza holds the Vaillancourt Fountain, a 40-foot-high, 710-ton sculpture with concrete chutes and a staircase to an observation platform. Canadian artist Armand Vaillancourt designed it in 1971 to mirror the unsightliness of the Embarcadero Freeway. Since the freeway no longer blights the bay and the city pays $250,000 per year to pump 30,000 gallons of water through the sculpture's chutes, there have been calls for its removal.

In the plaza you will find craft vendors (at the end of Market Street), two sculpted heads called *Yin & Yang*, the Abraham Lincoln Brigade memorial, inexpensive food, and a kiosk that relates the history of the Embarcadero with text and photos.

Cross the street back to the Embarcadero and continue walking northwest. At Pier 1½ a sign on top of a kiosk indicates "Herb Caen Way..." It runs from Harrison Street to Broadway and honors the newspaper columnist who earned the Pulitzer Prize for writing about his "cool, grey city of love" from 1938 to 1996.

Herb Caen Way

5. Pier 7 has been recreated with old-fashioned boards, benches, and lamps. Walk to the end to see the Transamerica Pyramid, the Ferry Building, and a closer view of Angel Island in the bay.

Pier 7

6. Pier 15 brings you to the Exploratorium, which boasts the latest in interactive science and technology for kids and adults. Plan to stay a minimum of 2.5 hours. There's a silent movie on the 1934 dock strike and if you walk around the pier there's no charge to see a wind harp and a model and history of the Bay Bridge.

Pier 15

Option: To see where Philo T. Farnsworth and his Lab Gang invented television, walk south and turn right on Green Street for a few blocks. At the corner of Sansome a plaque in a rock commemorates their achievement; No. 202 housed their laboratory. Retrace your steps to continue up the Embarcadero.

The Exploratorium

7. Pier 33 is where you take a boat to tour Alcatraz. Book at least a few days ahead or you will likely be disappointed. The pier contains some life-sized dioramas about the island's inhabitants: criminals, guards, and families.

Pier 33: Alcatraz cruise

8. Pier 39 is where sea lions flop on boat docks. To see them, walk toward the bay, skirting the restaurants to your right. You will also see good views of Alcatraz, the Golden Gate Bridge, Angel Island, Marin County's headlands (on the

Pier 39

Sea lions on the docks

View of Alcatraz from Pier 39

Pier 45: WWII ships

The Musée Mécanique

far side of the bridge), and Mount Tamalpais. Pier 39 is home to the Aquarium of the Bay and a raft of T-shirt and souvenir stores, eateries, and musicians (scheduled day and night). At the end of the pier sits the San Francisco Carousel. Hand carved in Italy and splashed with scenes of San Francisco, it claims to be the only carousel in the U. S. decorated with paintings of its home city.

Historic note: From 1853 to 1890s, Meiggs Wharf extended from Pier 39 to Fisherman's Wharf.

Option: Cross the street to Boudin Bakery & Café for a free self-tour and some sourdough bread or a meal.

9. From Pier 45 see a WWII Liberty ship christened the *S.S. Jeremiah O'Brien* and a submarine called the *Pampanito*—each for a fee. The Musée Mécanique is free and contains Edward Zelinsky's collection of arcade games, players, and movies from yesteryear, many from Playland at the Beach, an amusement park near Golden Gate Park, which closed in 1972. There's a vintage Kiss-o-meter, toothpick sculptures by a San Quentin inmate, 1906 earthquake footage, and more. To see the mechanical devices play, you need nickels, dimes, or quarters.

Pier 45 terminates the Embarcadero and leads to Fisherman's Wharf. Retrace your steps on Embarcadero to Taylor and turn right. Then make another right on Beach to Fisherman's Wharf.

10. Italian immigrants established San Francisco's fishing industry at Fisherman's Wharf in the late 1890s. As families opened

seafood stands, Fisherman's Wharf morphed into what it is now famous for: fish stands and seafood restaurants with great bay views that retain the names of the Italian fishing families. In addition, you can watch bakers making sourdough bread through a 30-foot window at Boudin's.

Fisherman's Wharf

Walk east and turn right on Beach and turn right again on Leavenworth to enter the brick Cannery building.

11. Built in 1907 to house the Fruit Packers Association, the Cannery became a Del Monte plant until 1968, when it was converted to a shopping center with footbridges and other passageways that lead to courtyards. Today it offers crafts, apparel, and ethnic shops, as well as restaurants.

Selling crabs at the Wharf

A courtyard with a pub separates the brick Cannery from the brick Haslett Warehouse, your next stop. To reach it, head north on Leavenworth and turn left on Jefferson—a journey of a few feet.

The Cannery

Note: The National Park Service runs #13–15 and has rangers available to help you.

12. The Haslett Warehouse, a historic landmark, contains the Maritime Visitor Center with exhibits about the history of the shipping industry, an antique Fresnel lighthouse lens, and a theater.

Courtyard

A few steps away, at Hyde and Jefferson, you'll find the Hyde Street Pier.

13. The Hyde Street Pier showcases a fleet of eight 19th- and early-20th-century ships—all for $5 for a seven-day ticket and free for those 15

The Haslett Warehouse

Hyde Street Pier

Aquatic Park

Aquatic Park Bathhouse Building

Buena Vista Café

Ghirardelli Square

and under accompanied by an adult. You can board and inspect *Balclutha,* an 1886 square-rigger; *Eureka,* an 1890 steam ferryboat; the *San Francisco Bay Ark,* circa 1890; *Alma,* an 1891 scow schooner; *C. A. Thayer,* an 1895 schooner; *Hercules,* a 1907 steam tugboat; *Eppleton Hall,* a 1914 paddlewheel tug; and *Wapama,* a 1915 steam schooner.

Next door is Aquatic Park where the Polar Bear Club meets. Members have swum to Alcatraz and back on occasion.

14. In full view is the Aquatic Park Bathhouse Building—the white, streamlined Art Deco building resembling an ocean liner. A joint project of the city and the WPA in 1939, the building was occupied by troops from 1941–8. In 1951 it opened as the first Senior Center in the United States. View WPA murals in the lobby and sculptures on the verandah. The San Francisco National Maritime Museum also occupies the building and has three floors of exhibits.

Go east on Beach Street. At the corner of Hyde Street is the Buena Vista Café.

15. Synonymous with Irish coffee, which its owner introduced to the U.S. in 1952, the Buena Vista Café also serves food.

Head south on Hyde and turn onto North Point and Ghirardelli Square.

16. Ghirardelli Square (pronounced Gear-ar-delly) was built in 1864 and operated as Pioneer Woolen Mill. In 1893 the expanding Ghirardelli Chocolate Company—founded by Gold Rush immigrant Domingo Ghirardelli—took it over. Bought out in the early 1960s,

the company moved across the bay. Desiring to protect the square from condominium development, shipping family members William Roth and his mother Lurline Matson Roth acquired the property in 1962. They instigated the first major adaptive re-use project in the U.S., re-purposing the square as a restaurant and retail space, which fully opened in 1965. Today Ghirardelli Square is a national landmark that retains the original clock tower building from 1915 along with the earlier Chocolate, Cocoa and Mustard buildings, which still sells its namesake's chocolate.

Ghirardelli Square clock tower

Cable Car Powell-Hyde line

GOLDEN GATE PARK AND HAIGHT-ASHBURY

Golden Gate Park contains 680 acres of forest, 130 acres of meadows, 330 acres of lakes, and only 15 miles of roadways. Scottish immigrant John McLaren designed and created the park, and served as the its superintendant for nearly 60 years. He abhorred buildings, memorials, and statues, so there are few, mostly obscured by greenery.

GOLDEN GATE PARK
1. Japanese Tea Garden
2. The de Young Museum
3. Music Concourse
4. California Academy of Sciences
5. National AIDS Memorial Grove
6. Conservatory of Flowers
7. McLaren Lodge

HAIGHT-ASHBURY
8. Panhandle Park
9. Red Victorian
10. Superba Theatre
11. Pall Mall Lounge
12. Psychedelic Shop
13. Jimi Hendrix Residence
14. Janis Joplin Residence
15. Joe McDonald Residence
16. Grateful Dead Residence
17. Hells Angels Headquarters
18. Masonic Street
19. Drogstore
20. Bound Together Bookstore
21. Buena Vista Park
22. 737 Buena Vista Avenue West

START:
Muni: Line 5, 21, 71

END:
Muni: Line 24, 33, 43, 71

TOUR TIME:
About 4 hours

CHAPTERS:
11, 13, 21, 25, 27

The park has hosted fairs (notably the 1894 Midwinter International Exposition, which brought in some permanent buildings including stops #1–3, and 6), refugees (40,000 lived in tents here following the 1906 quake), and youth (30,000 showed up at the old polo field for the Human Be-In in 1967), and it continues to offer a variety of events throughout the year.

The park presents many meanders, especially if you have a car. This tour hits the highlights, including the museums, and requires no vehicle.

Japanese Tea Garden

Drum Bridge

Pagoda

1. The Japanese Tea Garden contains paths and gardens including a ceremonial cypress gate, a moon bridge (a.k.a. a drum bridge) shaped to allow junk boats to sail under, and a pagoda (moved from the 1915 Panama–Pacific Expo). Its five acres of grounds also contain a Zen garden, a sunken garden, a Peace Lantern, koi ponds, a bronze Buddha, a ceremonial gate, and a tea pavilion where you can learn how to conduct a tea ceremony.

Initially built as part of the 1894 Midwinter International Expo, the Tea Garden proved such a hit that the city contracted its landscaper, merchant Makoto Hagiwara, to manage it and live on the premises with his family. He introduced fortune cookies to the U.S. at the tea house, and his family continued to oversee the garden until 1942. The garden fell into ruin during WWII with the forced removal of the Hagiwaras and other Japanese Americans to relocation camps. The gardens were eventually restored, but the city refused to revive its broken contract with the Hagiwaras.

Today the garden has three full-time gardeners and free admission on Mondays, Wednesdays, and Fridays before 10 a.m.

Turn left (northeast) on Hagiwara Tea Garden Drive. You'll see the Music Concourse Drive on your right and the de Young museum (at 50 Hagiwara Tea Garden Drive) on your left.

Japanese relocation, 1942

2. The original 1895 building here was damaged in the 1906 quake. The pseudo–Egyptian Revival-style building was repaired but was outgrown by its art collections. Michael de Young, co-founder of the *Chronicle* newspaper, commissioned a new building, which was completed in 1919 and named after him. The building deteriorated until 1989 when the Loma Prieta quake finished it off.

The de Young Museum

Swiss architects Herzog & de Meuron designed a new building, which opened in 2005. It is the largest copper-clad building in the world; its outer shell is composed of 475 tons of copper, designed to oxidize to a rich patina over time. Ride the elevator up the building's 144-foot Hamon Tower for free, where you'll find a gift shop and a city vista.

Sphinx and Hamon Tower

The de Young has special exhibits along with permanent collections of American, African, and Oceanic art, and draws more than 1.5 million visitors annually. Its landscaping includes a children's garden and sculpture garden along with palm trees dating back to the original 1895 building and the original Pool of Enchantment with vases and sphinxes.

Entrance area of the de Young

Cross the street to the Music Concourse, a park-like area with a bandshell.

3. The Music Concourse has three fountains,

View towards the Academy of Sciences from the de Young

Spreckles Temple of Music

Fountain in the Music Concourse

California Academy of Science

Indoor Rainforest

Shakespeare Garden

statues, and historical markers on the ground. The bandshell, known as the Spreckles Temple of Music or the Music Pavilion, hosts free concerts on Sundays, when many streets in Golden Gate Park are blocked off for pedestrians. You can rent bikes and Segways nearby. The London Plane trees lining the central concourse walkway have been pollarded—had their upper branches systematically pruned.

Opposite the Music Concourse from the de Young Museum is the California Academy of Sciences.

4. Designed by architect Renzo Piano, the $488-million green building opened in 2008. Its 2.5 acre living roof supports 1.7 million native plants. Inside are 900 species of animals—38,000 in total. The academy also holds Kimball Natural History Museum, Morrison Planetarium, Steinhart Aquarium, African Hall, and a four-story rainforest dome. It covers 11 scientific fields, features educational programs, and is open daily.

Facing the Music Concourse from the front of the Academy of Sciences, turn left. Follow the walkway until it ends at 19th Avenue (which has no sign). Turn left. Pass the entrance to the Shakespeare Garden (a quick detour if you like), then turn left on Nancy Pelosi Drive (Middle East Drive on older maps). At the intersection with Bowling Green Drive you will see the National AIDS Memorial Grove.

5. Members of the community devastated by AIDS transformed a dilapidated dell into a serene space dedicated to those affected by AIDS. In 1996 Congress designated it the National AIDS Memorial Grove.

Return to Nancy Pelosi Drive and turn right. When you reach John F. Kennedy Drive you'll see a large glass conservatory across the street. Cross JFK and follow the pathway to the conservatory.

6. Modeled after the greenhouse at London's Kew Gardens and opened in 1879, the Conservatory of Flowers is the oldest glass-and-wood Victorian greenhouse in the Western Hemisphere. A living museum comprised of four galleries—Lowland Tropics, Highland Tropics, Aquatics, and Potted Plant—it's home to carnivorous plants, rare orchids, century-old philodendron, and lily pads. The conservatory has been saved from rot and the wrecking ball several times. Admission is free the first Tuesday of each month.

Haight-Ashbury

The Haight, as the neighborhood is known locally, once consisted of sand dunes, prompting the Spanish to dub it "Tierra de las Pulgas" (Land of the Fleas). When cable cars began running to the area in 1883, it became a weekend getaway and the streets got their names: Haight after exchange banker Henry Haight and Ashbury after Board of Supervisors member Munroe Ashbury, who helped create Golden Gate Park.

The Depression and WWII hit the Haight hard. Houses became shabby and cheap, ripe for youth who flocked in during the '60s, bringing their free spirits, music, drugs, and beliefs. Haight-Ashbury became the epicenter of the counterculture that drew 100,000 young people in 1967 alone. Soon, the days of high spirits were over. Many got strung out on drugs, making the Haight a dangerous place during the 1970s.

National AIDS Memorial Grove

Conservatory of Flowers

Park map

Stanyan and Haight streets, 1887

Sunday afternoon in Golden Gate Park, c. 1902

Haight Ashbury Free Clinic, 1967

"Death of the Hippie" parade, 1967

McLaren Lodge

Panhandle Park

Jimi Hendrix at the Park, 1967

Like Puff the Magic Dragon, the 1960s hippie counterculture has vanished, but a few signs of flower power remain in the Haight. First, there's the continuation of HIP (Haight Independent Proprietors), a local merchant association. This means few chain stores (Ben and Jerry's is present, but gives 10 percent to the community). Also, a few of the original stores and signage from the era are still around. A tour of the Haight allows you to sense the 1960s, and view the district's decked out Victorians.

7. To reach Haight-Ashbury from the conservatory of Flowers in Golden Gate Park, turn left (east) on JFK. To your right you can see Hippie Hill, where members of the counterculture hung out. Moving along JFK, on your left you will see a brownstone Mission Revival-style building: McLaren Lodge. Constructed in 1896 to house Park Superintendant John McLaren, it's now the headquarters of the Recreation and Parks Department and has free maps of the park.

Continue on JFK and cross Stanyon Street— the border of the park and Haight-Ashbury— to enter the park at the western tip of the Panhandle, an eight-block swath of greenery.

8. As you ramble in Panhandle Park, notice the variety of trees—McLaren tested plantings here. Also, notice the one-way street that runs by the park to the south: Oak Street. Lined with Victorians, Oak is where the Haight's streets dead end. Make a note of where Cole Street dead ends at Oak, as you will return there to continue your tour.

During the 1960s, the Grateful Dead, Jefferson Airplane, Santana, Jimi Hendrix, and many other local musicians regularly played in Panhandle Park. Hippies panhandled on Stanyan, though the term predates the 1960s and has no connection to the park.

Haight Street

Cross Oak Street and proceed on Cole to Haight Street and turn right.

Haight Street's vibe is low-key, with an abundance of cafés, music stores, pubs, boutiques, and memorabilia shops.

The Red Victorian

9. 1665 Haight: The Red Victorian opened in 1904 as the Jefferson Inn, a getaway resort. During the 1960s it became a crash pad known as the Jeffrey-Haight. In 1977 environmental artist and social activist Sami Sunchild purchased the building and restored it. Today, it's a B&B and home to the Peaceful World Foundation, Peace Center, Peace Arts Gallery, and a Peace Café.

Superba Theatre

10. 1660 Haight: Across the street at No. 1660 is the Art Nouveau-style Superba Theatre (currently Wasteland, a vintage clothing store), which was originally built as a nickelodeon called the Sunset Theater.

Former Pall Mall Lounge

11. 1568 Haight: In the late '60s, an Iranian woman nicknamed "Love" by her customers ran the short-order counter here at what was then the Pall Mall Lounge. She repaid them by creating Love Burgers, charging from 0–25¢ depending on the person's pocketbook. People lined up for blocks for the free burgers she doled out on holidays.

Psychedelic Shop, 1967

12. 1535 Haight: Ron and Jay Thelin ran the Psychedelic Shop here from January 1966

1524 Haight Street

Haight and Ashbury streets

635 Ashbury Street

Janis Joplin

638 Ashbury Street

to October 1967. It carried albums, incense, posters, concert tickets, books, etc. After too many tourists gawked in the window at the hippies, the Thelins put seats in the window so locals could stare back. Presently the place is a pizza shop.

13. 1524 Haight Street: A mural of Jimi Hendrix on the east side of the building marks his upstairs apartment.

Now you will arrive at the famous intersection of Haight and Ashbury. Notice the shop at the northwest corner. A square clock hangs from it, frozen at 4:20 because 420 is a euphemism for marijuana. The Haight Ashbury Free Clinic is near the north corner at 558 Clayton Street.

Turn right on Ashbury.

Ashbury Street boasts some pretty Victorian "Painted Ladies" as well as a few famous former residents.

14. 635 Ashbury: Janis Joplin lived here among many other places in the Haight.

15. 638 Ashbury: Country Joe McDonald lived here.

16. 710 Ashbury: In 1890 the elite architectural team of Cranston-Keenan designed this Queen Anne-style house. Thanks to the largesse of Owsley Stanley, "the chemist" who made the best and safest LSD and paid the rent, the Grateful Dead lived here from October 1966 to March 1968. Colored photos of band members embedded in sidewalk mark the house. The band paid tribute to Stanley—a large man nicknamed "Bear"—by designing their icon after him.

On October 2, 1967, the narc squad staged a bust on the house with a dozen reporters and TV crews in tow. They arrested band members Pigpen, Bob Weir, and nine others for possession of marijuana. The case hit the national spotlight when *Rolling Stone* reported it in its first issue on November 9, 1967. Charges were later dropped.

710 Ashbury Street

17. 719 Ashbury: This unnumbered house between No. 715 and No. 721 was the Hells Angels headquarters. The Angels bonded with the Dead and provided security in the Haight.

The Grateful Dead at 710 Ashbury

Retrace your steps on Ashbury and turn right on Waller. Follow Waller to Masonic and turn left.

18. Masonic Street contains some eye-popping Victorians such as those at 1226–38 and 1250–56. They were built from 1895 to 1896 by Cranston and Keenan. In 1974 and 1975 the SLA (Symbionese Liberation Army) periodically hid with their captive Patty Hearst at 1235 Masonic.

719 Ashbury Street

19. When you get to Haight, turn right. Before proceeding, notice the building at the northeast corner: 1398 Haight Street. This café and counterculture meeting spot was called the Drogstore because the fuzz (police) forbade the owners to name it the Drugstore.

1250 and 1256 Masonic Street

Continue on Haight to Buena Vista Park.

20. On the way, at 1369 Haight, you will pass the Bound Together Bookstore, run by an anarchist collective since 1976. A mural of famous U.S. anarchists against a background of books on shelves decorates the outside wall. Run by volunteers, the bookstore is stocked with radical books, comics, and magazines.

The Drogstore

Bound Together Bookstore

Mural on Haight Street

Central Avenue near the park

Buena Vista Park

"Death of Money" parade, 1966

Proceed to Buena Vista Park, which will be on your right.

21. Pried away from squatters who were paid to leave, Hill Park was established in 1867. In 1894 its 36 acres were renamed and dedicated as Buena Vista Park, and it became the city's third largest park. Golden Gate Park Superintendant John McLaren oversaw the forestation of its sand dunes with plantings that made for the thickly wooded park that exists today. After the 1906 quake, people gathered on its summit to observe the fires.

The 1960s saw many gatherings in Buena Vista Park as hippies hung out here. In 1967 the park was the terminus for a solemn, political event instigated by the Diggers, an activist, anarchist collective. The Diggers were known for their Free Store (where everything was free), their Digger Stew (also free and vegetarian), and their 1966 "Death of Money" parade. They felt the media created and derided the hippie. The Gray Line Bus Company's Hippie Hop tours—promoted as "the only foreign tour within the continental limits of the United States"—exacerbated this sentiment and caused Diggers and residents alike to act out in front of the gaping tourists. So the Diggers organized the "Death of the Hippie" parade to end the media's portrayal of, and profit from, hippies. In early October 1967, they carried a coffin down Haight Street with an effigy of a hippie inside. They buried the hippie along with the sign to the Psychedelic Shop in Buena Vista Park.

The park continues to be a gathering place. You can hike up the 575-foot hill for excellent city views, navigate its perimeter by a circular sidewalk, or hang out on the grass.

To enter the park, walk down Haight to Lyon Street where steps will lead you up.

22. If you choose to walk the perimeter, at the intersection of Lyon and Buena Vista Avenue East, notice the two elaborate Victorians and flat-iron building at the corners. Also, at 737 Buena Vista Avenue West is the Spreckels mansion, a Queen Anne-Colonial Revival house built in 1897 by sugar king Claus Spreckels for his nephew. The place has had many illustrious residents including writers Ambrose Bierce and Jack London, who penned *White Fang* here. Graham Nash (of Crosby, Stills, Nash & Young) bought it and turned it into a recording studio where many musicians cut albums in the 1960s and 1970s. San Francisco-born actor Danny Glover acquired the mansion in the 1990s.

View from the park

737 Buena Vista Avenue West

CASTRO AND MISSION

Twin Peaks, the two 922-foot-high hills at the center of the city, sent two streams—Eureka and Noe—down their slopes, which named two adjacent neighborhoods: Eureka Valley and Noe Valley. Unscathed by the 1906 quake and fires, the Eureka Valley neighborhood—now called the Castro—was blue-collar for decades, predominantly Irish Catholics, along with Germans and Scandinavians. Over the years they shifted to the suburbs. Beginning in the mid '60s gay men

CASTRO
1. Harvey Milk Plaza
2. Twin Peaks Tavern
3. Castro Theatre
4. Cliff's Variety Store
5. GLBT History Museum
6. Most Holy Redeemer Catholic Church
7. Metropolitan Community Church

8. Harvey Milk Civil Rights Academy
9. Human Rights Campaign Store (formerly Castro Camera)

MISSION
10. Dolores Park
11. Mission Dolores

Haight St.
Waller St.
Germania St.
Herman St.
Lloyd St.
Duboce Park
Duboce Ave.
Buena Vista Park
MUNI Metro
Alpine Terrace
Divisadero St.
Castro St.
Noe St.
Walter St.
Sanchez St.
Belcher St.
Church St.
Dolores St.
14th St.
Henry St.
15th St.
Landers St.
Alert Aly
Corona Heights Park
Beaver St.
MUNI Metro
Sharon St.
16th St.
Chula Ln.
Market St.
Pond St.
Prosper St.
CASTRO
MISSION
17th St.
Dorland
Ford St.
Hartford St.
18th St.
Mission Dolores Park
Hancock St.
Eureka Valley Rec Center
19th St.
Cumberland St.
Kite Hill Open Space
Diamond St.
Collingswood St.
EUREKA VALLEY
20th St.
Liberty St.
Eureka St.
21st St.
Chattanooga St.
Hill St.
22nd St.
Vicksburg St.
Alvardo St.
23rd St.
Mersey
Elizabeth St.
NOE VALLEY
24th St.
Jersey St.
25th St.
Clipper St.
26th St.
Cesar Chavez St.

START:
BART: 16th St/Mission
Muni: Line 24, 33, F, K, L, M, T

END:
BART: 16th St/Mission
Muni: Line 22 ,33, F, J, K, L, M, N, T

TOUR TIME:
About 3 hours

CHAPTERS:
1, 26, 27

Harvey Milk Plaza

Photos at the plaza

Pink Triangle Park

trickled in, attracted by the cheap rents and prices for the rundown Italianate Edwardian houses left behind.

Today the Castro continues to be a neighborhood wrapped around a commercial core centered at Castro and Eighteenth Street.

1. Start at Harvey Milk Plaza at the intersection of Market and Castro next to the Muni station whose entryway displays plaques with scenes from Milk's life. Nothing proclaims the Castro and gay pride better than this corner of concrete with its rainbow flag—a universal symbol for gays and lesbians—originally designed for the 1978 Gay Freedom parade by Gilbert Baker. From here marches have started, most famously the November 27, 1978, candlelight march that occurred spontaneously hours after ex-Supervisor Dan White assassinated Supervisor Harvey Milk and Mayor George Moscone.

Observe the trompe l'oeil painting on the wall of a house with a tower.

Walk west to the corner of Collingwood.

a) Look north across two streets to see the house that inspired the trompe l'oeil mural.

b) Across the street, see Pink Triangle Park. Consisting of a rose garden, 15 granite posts, and a triangle made of rose quartz, it memorializes homosexuals murdered and imprisoned by the Nazi regime during World War II.

Walk east to Castro and cross to Twin Peaks Tavern.

2. In 1972 two lesbians bought this pre-Prohibition bar and let the sun shine through the previously obscured full-length windows, reflecting the movement of gays and lesbians out of the shadows. In 2013 the tavern was designated a landmark, one of only two bars in the city to earn this status. Today it hosts old and young and is a place to eat, drink, socialize, and see and be seen through its transformational windows.

Twin Peaks Tavern

Continue on Castro to the Castro Theatre.

3. The Castro Theatre is an art house and landmark, it also hosts film festivals and events such as the world premiere of *Milk* in 2008. Conceived to resemble a Mexican cathedral on the exterior, its elaborate interior includes a Mighty Wurlitzer pipe organ that plays before movies and events.

Castro Theatre

Castro Theatre

Continue on Castro to Cliff's Variety store.

4. Since 1936 the family-owned Cliff's Variety store had moved around the neighborhood, before settling here and annexing the building next door. It stocks everything from hardware items to housewares to fun and sexy gifts and always sports a playful window display.

Castro Theatre entrance

Continue on Castro to 18th Street: the Castro's central crossroads.

Notice Harvey's Bar across the street. Until 1990 it was called the Elephant Walk. After Dan White was convicted of involuntary manslaughter and given a 7-year sentence for killing Milk and Moscone on May 21,

Cliff's Variety

Playful window display

Harvey's Bar

Castro Street

GLBT History Museum

Most Holy Redeemer Catholic Church

1979, the White Night riots occurred. Gays and supporters marched and wreaked havoc, smashing police vehicles and setting them on fire. Covering their badges, the cops retaliated by clubbing people at the Civic Center and in the Castro and trashing the Elephant Walk, beating patrons and employees. With 100 protestors and 61 cops hospitalized and 24 arrests, the police chief finally ordered his troops off the streets. The damage totaled more than $1 million.

Optional: Continue to No. 518 Castro: the Under One Roof store. This nonprofit shop stocks interesting, amusing, and retro items, and donates 100 percent of the proceeds to community-based HIV/AIDS organizations. Retrace your steps to 18th Street.

Walk west on 18th Street to No. 4127 and the GLBT History Museum (the first in the U.S.).

5. For a small fee you can view the GLBT History Museum's current exhibit as well as its permanent collection, which includes Milk artifacts such as a "Harvey Milk for Supervisor" T-shirt and the pantsuits Del Martin and Phyllis Lyon wore in 2008 when Mayor Newsome presided and they became the city's first legally married same-sex couple.

Continue west on 18th and turn left on Diamond Street.

6. Most Holy Redeemer Catholic Church has occupied 100 Diamond Street since 1901 and served the Irish Catholic community for years. When that community left and gays appeared, the church was unwelcoming and almost closed. In the 1980s two open-minded pastors appeared and welcomed everyone. They

formed "Gays and Grays," a group of longtime parishioners—mostly grandmothers—who cared for abandoned, AIDS-stricken men and created an AIDS hospice. Today drag queens and transgender people regularly attend services alongside straights.

Retrace your steps to 18th Street and turn left. Turn left at the next street—Eureka—and continue until No. 150 and the Metropolitan Community Church (MCC).

7. Formed in 1970 as a church for GLBT people, the San Francisco MCC first met in a North Beach bar. Led by eight ministers, the church met at different locations, one of which was firebombed, until settling in this building in 1980. AIDS decimated the church's membership, and MCC buried people when other religious institutions wouldn't and often held memorial services. The MCC has also given marijuana to ill people. Today the church continues its activist work with the motto "Diverse beliefs. Common values. A home for queer spirituality." It is one of 222 MCC congregations in 37 countries.

Continue on Eureka and turn left on 19th Street to find No. 4235: the Harvey Milk Civil Rights Academy.

8. Formerly called the Douglass School, this alternative public elementary school was renamed Harvey Milk Civil Rights Academy in 1996. When Milk was in office in 1978, the number of students here dwindled due to the childless gay population. Believing in education and that the Castro should be a community for all, Milk successfully fought its closure. Notice the students' colorful murals and their hopeful messages.

Metropolitan Community Church

Street in front of the church

Harvey Milk Civil Rights Academy

Students murals

Eureka Valley Recreation Center facing the Academy

Billy dolls

Cheeky window display

HRC store

Harvey Milk at Castro Camera

Mission Dolores, 1851

Continue on 19th for a block and a half and cross Castro to its southeast corner. If nudity doesn't bother you, study the Billy dolls in the window. Discontinued and selling for upwards of $200 on eBay, the dolls created by this apartment's resident make some sly, political statements with their attire and the flags they wave.

9. Cross 19th and head north on Castro to No. 575: the store of the Human Rights Campaign (HRC, the largest national advocacy organization for GLBT rights). A bronze plaque in the sidewalk informs you that this store was originally Castro Camera, the business Harvey Milk ran with his partner Scott Smith from 1972 until Milk's murder in 1978. They lived above the store, which also functioned as a community hangout and Milk's campaign headquarters.

Learn more about Milk and GLBT history here and purchase Milk and HRC merchandise. In 2000 the City Planning Commission made the store a historic landmark.

This ends your tour of the Castro. Try Castro's eating establishments, bars, or stores before continuing to the Mission tour, which offers none unless you walk a little farther.

Mission

The Yelamu tribe of the Ohlone Indians inhabited Chutchui Village in the area until 1776 when Spanish Catholics established a mission here. The next settlers in "The Mission," as the area has been called ever since, were the gold seekers in 1849. By 1900, working-class Irish, Italians, Scandinavians, and Germans occupied the Mission district. As they relocated after World War II, new immigrants from Mexico and Central America moved in. The Mission's latest arrivals have been the Internet professionals who showed up during the 1990s and are gentrifying the neighborhood. Walk back on Castro and turn left (east) on 19th Street. Continue on 19th to Dolores Park.

Dolores Park

10. The location of many a rally, the 13.7-acre Dolores Park was fittingly named after El Grito de Dolores, the famous rallying cry of Miguel Hidalgo, the father of Mexican independence. From 1861 until 1894 two synagogues owned the park and buried their dead in the upper southwest corner. (They were re-interred in Colma, a town to the south, along with most of San Francisco's dead.) The city bought the land in 1905. In 1906, after the quake and its fires devastated the Mission district, 1,600 families paid rent to tent in the park for two years.

Jewish cemetery, 1880

After the quake, 1906

The park has seen many rock concerts and protests. The Sisters of Perpetual Indulgence celebrate their anniversary in it every year with outlandish costumes and contests. It also has a children's playground and city views.

a) Turn right on Church Street. At 20th, find the Little Giant Gold Hydrant. One of a few hydrants that operated after the quake, it was worth its weight in gold when it helped save the 20th to 22nd street blocks from fires. Every year on the April 18, to honor its contribution, the hydrant receives a fresh coat of gold paint.

Little Giant Gold Hydrant

b) Walk diagonally into the park and view the bronze statue of Miguel Hidalgo.

Statue of Miguel Hidalgo

Replica of Mexico's liberty bell

Mission Dolores

Mission Dolores, 1856

William Leidesdorff's grave

New basilica (right), 1918

c) Cross the park to Dolores Avenue to see a replica of Mexico's liberty bell, gifted by the Mexican government in 1966 to commemorate Mexican Independence Day on September 16.

Exit the park and head north on Dolores Avenue to Mission Dolores at the corner of 16th Street. (You'll pass Mission High School on your left after you cross 18th Street.)

11. Mission Dolores (Mission San Francisco de Asís), the oldest building in the city, was erected in 1776 by Franciscan missionaries. Pay the low admission fee and take the self-guided tour to learn more about the mission complex, the missionaries, and the Yelamu. Don't miss the stone in the floor of the first chapel you enter that marks William Leidesdorff's grave. In the tiny graveyard (it is the city's oldest) a redwood grave marker, recently created in the original style, honors a Yelamu couple.

Your tour ends here. If you'd like to experience more of the Mission's culture and taste Mexican, Peruvian, El Salvadorian, and other cuisines, walk south on Dolores back past to the park. Turn left on 18th and walk a few blocks to Mission Avenue—the district's main street—and turn right. Stroll on Mission until you see a restaurant you like.

Mission San Francisco de Asis, Mission & Sixteenth Streets, before 1835

GOLDEN GATE BRIDGE, PRESIDIO, AND PALACE OF FINE ARTS

This tour involves more walking and fewer stops than the others, but is exhilarating since it takes you close to the Golden Gate Bridge and the bay and then farther away for unbeatable views.

START:
Muni: Line 28, 29, 43

END:
Muni: Line 30

TOUR TIME:
About 4 hours

CHAPTERS:
1, 14, 16, 20

1. Begin at the San Francisco side of the iconic Golden Gate Bridge. You will see a square with three buildings: Bridge Café, Bridge Pavilion (souvenirs and tours), and Bridge Roundhouse (tours, food, a fake bridge background for photos). There are also kiosks and a bronze stand with historical info and PresidiGo, a free shuttle van that stops all around the Presidio.

Option: Take the walkway across the Golden Gate Bridge. It is 1.8 miles to the other side to a Vista Point with statues and information. Walking even part way can be thrilling.

To get to the next stop—Fort Point, beneath the bridge—take a semi-circular trail that loops down to the bay and back toward the bridge. (Part way down you will see signs for Fort Point that you can follow, but here are the directions as well.) Begin by walking northeast on the Vista Access and turn left on the walkway. Bear left onto Andrew Road for a short distance and bear left on the walkway for .6 miles. When you get to Marine Drive turn left. (Note for later: A right turn takes you onto Crissy Field.) You will see Fort Point, which is .3 miles farther.

Square at Golden Gate Bridge

View of the Golden Gate Bridge

Follow the signs for Fort Point

Note: Stops #1-4 are run by the National Park Service (NPS) and part of the GGNRA (Golden Gate National Recreation Area) and are free.

2. In 1853 at the height of the Gold Rush, the U.S. Army Corps of Engineers began construction of Fort Point, the only masonry type of fort west of the Mississippi. Completed in 1861, just in time for the Civil War, when the fort was occupied by the Army and deterred Confederates from attacking the West Coast.

Today Fort Point functions as a fort and a museum. You can take free guided or self-guided tours. You can also visit its "Powder Room" and, starting at noon, watch a cannon-loading drill. The NPS also sponsors events such as candlelight tours from November through February (reservations required).

Retrace your steps on Marine Drive to where you turned left. Now go right onto Crissy Field.

3. For centuries Crissy Field was a 130-acre tidal marsh and estuary where the Yelamu tribe fished. When the Spanish arrived in 1776, they grazed livestock and planted crops on it. In U.S. hands starting in 1846, the area came under Army control, first as a dumping ground. From the 1870s on, it was drained and covered over, finishing in time to hold the 1915 Panama–Pacific International Expo. With WWI it came under Air Force control and was named after Major Dana H. Crissy, a base commander and pilot who died in 1919 on a test flight from the field.

In 1994, when the Army transferred the Presidio and Crissy Field to the NPS, it was a mix of concrete, asphalt, and derelict buildings. Foundations and the public contributed 34.5 million dollars and many volunteer hours to return Crissy Field to a natural condition and make it an urban national park. More than 87 tons of hazardous waste, 75 tons of rubble, and 70 acres of asphalt were removed. Lagoons were re-created, plants planted, walkways laid down, and buildings restored and re-purposed. This work continues since Crissy Field's re-opening in 2001.

Crissy Field offers bay views and a beach, the Warming Hut bookstore and café with souvenirs and picnic benches, and info kiosks. Nearby is the Farallones Marine Sanctuary

Fort Point

Fort Point scene, *Vertigo*, 1958

Crissy Field

Crissy Field, c. 1920s

Tidal marsh

The bridge seen from Crissy Field

Airial view of the Presidio

Presidio, c. 1815

San Francisco National Cemetery

Old brick barracks

Visitor Center, a museum with tanks of local sea creatures.

Your next stop takes you to the historic former military base—the Presidio—where your first stop is a cemetery. From the Farallones Marine Sanctuary Visitor Center, walk away from the bay across Crissy Field toward the freeway and Mason Street, which parallels the bay. Locate 920 Mason, which is at a stop sign, and turn right, away from the bay. At the next stop sign turn left on Crissy Field Avenue. It becomes MacDowell Avenue, which takes you under the freeway. Turn left on Lincoln Boulevard and walk to the San Francisco National Cemetery on your right.

4. Dating from 1884, the cemetery expanded with war and over time to hold the remains of 30,000 veterans and their families on 29 acres. Buffalo soldiers from the Spanish-American War of the 1890s rest here, as do Civil War generals, Pauline Cushman-Frye (a Union spy), and Major Dana Crissy. Veterans from all major wars are interred here, although in 1973 the graveyard stopped burials except in reserved gravesites.

Continue on Lincoln Boulevard. Then continue onto Sheridan Avenue. Turn left on to Montgomery Street. Old brick barracks will be on your left and the Main Post lawn (the parade ground) on your right. Go to the last barracks (No. 105): the Presidio Visitor Center.

5. Currently the Visitor Center consists of a small museum with a sampling of Presidio history. A ranger is on duty with information about tours and to explain the map of the Presidio's trails and sites.

Retrace your steps up Montgomery Street to the next barracks, No. 104: the Walt Disney Family Museum.

Officers' Club

6. Created by Disney's daughter and grandson, run by the nonprofit Walt Disney Family Foundation and charging a hefty fee, the Walt Disney Family Museum chronicles the life of Walt Disney from his early life to his creation of Mortimer (Mickey) Mouse and the animation of Snow White, Bambi, Pinocchio, and other classic characters. The museum has videos, listening devices, and interactive exhibits, and provides a fascinating look at early animation and Disney's struggles. It features a 13-foot model of Disneyland as Disney imagined it. Allow four hours to see it all. The museum store (featuring unusual and vintage Disney items) and café are open to non-visitors as is the *Fantasia*-themed theater that projects Disney movies.

Walt Disney Family Museum

13-foot Model of Disneyland

To get to your next stop, continue to retrace your steps on Montgomery Street and turn right on Lincoln Boulevard. Then turn slight left onto the walkway and proceed northeast through the Presidio. Turn right onto Edie Road. Turn left onto the walkway and east through the Presidio. Stay straight to go onto Gorgas Avenue. Turn slight right onto Lyon Street and continue to the Palace of Fine Arts at 3301 Lyon.

Display at the Disney Museum

7. The open-air Palace of Fine Arts is an iconic SF building fought for, preserved, and entirely reconstructed since its creation out of chicken wire and plaster for the 1915 Panama–Pacific International Expo. Seagulls alight and swans and ducks paddle in its surrounding lagoon. There are six information stops around the palace's circumference that can be viewed

Palace of Fine Arts

Inside of Palace of Fine Arts

1915 Panama-Pacific Expo

Marina

Alcatraz over the Wave Organ

Wave Organ

in any order. As you stroll around, keep architect Bernard Maybeck's intentions in mind, which were to design "a Greek temple in the middle of a small mountain lake" that would evoke "an old Roman ruin, away from civilization."

If you'd like to walk through the tony Marina district and end your tour at the ocean at the world's only Wave Organ, take this .6 mile walk.

Leave from the north end of the palace and make a slight left onto Baker Street. Stay straight to go onto the walkway. Walk north through the Golden Gate National Recreation Area. Turn right onto Yacht Road until it ends. Continue walking—you'll pass a beach below on your right—until you reach a jetty jutting out in the bay where there's a good view of Alcatraz. Amidst the jagged jumble of jetty rocks and granite tombstones left from a Victorian graveyard, look for the Wave Organ, which was installed in 1986.

8. Once you discover the Wave Organ, hold your ear up to any of its 25 concrete pipes and wait. Mother Nature will play a faint or loud percussive concerto, depending on the tides—high tide at a full moon is best—on this acoustic sculpture. Waves activate the organ as "it's exposed to dynamic waters," reveals its designer, artist Peter Richards. "It's neither land nor water, but something in between."

INDEX

BIBLIOGRAPHY

Accardi, Catherine A. *San Francisco's North Beach and Telegraph Hill*, Arcadia Publishing, SF, CA: 2010.

Bowen, Robert W. and Bowen, Brenda Young. *San Francisco's Chinatown*, Arcadia Publishing, SF, CA: 2008.

Brechin, Gray. *Imperial San Francisco*, University of California Press, Berkeley, CA: 1999.

Bright, Beckey. "Where Are They: Jane Metcalfe," *Wall Street Journal*, May 5, 2006.

Browning, Peter. *Yerba Buena San Francisco: From the Beginning to the Gold Rush: 1769-1849*, Wild West Books, Lafayette, CA: 1998.

Camp, William M. *San Francisco: Ports of Gold*, Doubleday, Garden City, NY: 1947.

Chalmers, Claudine. *French San Francisco*, Arcadia Publishing, SF, CA: 2007.

Charyn, Jerome. *Joe DiMaggio: The Long Vigil*, Yale University Press, New Haven, CT: 2011.

Chinn, Thomas W. *Bridging the Pacific, San Francisco Chinatown and its People*, Chinese Historical Society of America, SF, CA: 1989.

Cohen, Katherine Powell. *San Francisco's Haight-Ashbury*, Arcadia Publishing, SF, CA: 2008.

Cohen, Katherine Powell. *San Francisco's Nob Hill*, Arcadia Publishing, SF, CA: 2010.

Conrad, Barnaby and Vernier, Carole. *The World of Herb Caen: San Francisco 1938-1997*, Chronicle Books, SF, CA: 1997.

Cornfield, Scott. *Children of Alcatraz*, DVD. Center for Nonprofit Media, Pleasanton, CA: 2003.

Coyote, Peter. *Sleeping Where I Fall*, Counterpoint: Washington DC: 1998.

Dickson, Samuel. *Tales of San Francisco*, Stanford University Press, Palo Alto, CA: 1992.

Dillon, Richard H. *North Beach: The Italian Heart of San Francisco*, Presidio Press, Novato, CA: 1985.

Echeverria, Emiliano and Rice, Walter. *San Francisco's Powell Street Cable Cars*, Arcadia Publishing, SF, CA: 2005.

Federal Writers' Project. *The WPA Guide to California*, Pantheon Books, NY, NY: 1939.

Fradkin, Philip L. *The Great Earthquake and Firestorms of 1906: How San Francisco Nearly Destroyed Itself*, University of California Press, Berkeley, CA: 2005.

Gaar, Gregg and Miller, Ryder W. *San Francisco: A Natural History*, Arcadia Publishing, SF, CA: 2006.

Garvey, John and California Center for Military History. *San Francisco in World War II*, Arcadia Publishing, SF, CA: 2007.

Girlich, Katherine Powell. *San Francisco Zoo*, Arcadia Publishing, SF, CA: 2009.

Graham, Bill and Greenfield, Robert. *Bill Graham Presents: My Life Inside Rock and Out*, Doubleday, NY, NY: 1992.

Holliday, JS. *Rush for Riches: Gold Fever and the Making of California*, Oakland Museum of California and University of California Press, Berkeley, CA: 1999.

Holmes, Eugenia Kellogg. *Adolph Sutro: A Brief Story of a Brilliant Life*, Press of San Francisco Photo-Engraving Company, SF, CA: 1895

Hooper, Bernadette C. *San Francisco's Mission District*, Arcadia Publishing, SF, CA: 2006.

Hudson, Lynn M. *The Making of "Mammy Pleasant": A Black Entrepreneur in Nineteenth-Century San Francisco*, University of Chicago Press, Chicago, IL: 2003.

Japantown Task Force, Inc. *San Francisco's Japantown*, Arcadia Publishing, SF, CA: 2005.

Lemke, Gayle. *The Art of the Fillmore: The Poster Series 1966-1971*, Thunder's Mouth Press, NY, NY: 2005.

Lewis, Oscar. *Bay Window Bohemia: An Account of the Brilliant Artistic World of Gaslit San Francisco*, Doubleday, Garden City, NY: 1956.

Lipsky, Dr. William. *Gay and Lesbian San Francisco*, Arcadia Publishing, SF, CA: 2006.

McGloin, John B. *San Francisco: The Story of a City*, Presidion Press, San Rafael, CA: 1978.

Lipsky, Dr. William. *San Francisco's Panama-Pacific International Exposition*, Arcadia Publishing, SF, CA: 2005.

Michaels, Leonard, David Reid, and Raquel Sher, editors. *West of the West: Imagining California*, North Point Press: SF, CA: 1989.

Mungo, Ray. *San Francisco Confidential*, Birch Lane Press, NY, NY: 1995.

Murphy, Bill. *A Pictorial History of California*, Fearon: SF, CA: 1958.

Muscatine, Doris. *Old San Francisco: The Biography of a City from Early Days to the Earthquake*, GP Putnam and Sons: NY, NY: 1975.

Narell, Irene. *Our City: The Jews of San Francisco*, Howell-North Books, San Diego, CA: 1981.

Ngai, Mae. *The Lucky Ones: One Family and the Extraordinary Invention of Chinese America*, Houghton Mifflin Harcourt, Boston: 2010.

O'Reilly, James, Larry Habegger, Sean O'Reilly, editors. *Travelers' Tales: San Francisco*, Travelers' Tales Inc., SF, CA: 1996.

Packer, George. "Change the World," *The New Yorker*, May 27, 2013.

Perry, Charles. *The Haight-Ashbury: A History*, Random House, NY, NY: 1984.

Rourke, Constance. *Troupers of the Gold Coast, or the Rise of Lotta Crabtree*, Harcourt, Brace and Company, NY, NY: 1928.

Shepard, Susan. *The Neighborhoods: A Guide to the Joys and Discoveries of San Francisco's Neighborhoods*, Chronicle Books, SF, CA: 1981.

Shilts, Randy. *And the Band Played On: Politics, People, and the AIDS Epidemic*, St. Martin's Press: NY, NY: 1987.

Shilts, Randy. *The Mayor of Castro Street: The Life and Times of Harvey Milk*, St. Martin's Press, NY, NY: 1982.

Sinclair, Mick. *San Francisco: A Cultural History*, Interlink Books, Northampton, MA: 2004.

Solnit, Rebecca. *Infinite City: A San Francisco Atlas*, University of California Press: Berkeley, CA: 2012.

Soulé, Frank, John H. Gihon, M.D., and James Nisbet. *Gold Rush: The Annals of San Francisco*, D. Appleton & Company, San Francisco, CA: 1855.

Starr, Kevin. *California: A History*, Modern Library, NY, NY: 2005.

Starr, Kevin. *Coast of Dreams: California on the Edge 1990-2003*, Alfred A. Knopf, NY, NY: 2004.

St. John, David. *An Emperor Among Us: The Eccentric Life and Benevolent Reign of Norton I, Emperor of the*

United States, as Told by Mark Twain, iUniverse, Bloomington, Indiana: 2012

Stone, Irving. *Men to Match My Mountains: The Opening of the Far West 1840-1900*, Castle Books, Secaucus, NJ: 2009.

Ute, Grant, Philip Hoffman, Cameron Beach, Robert Townley, and Walter

Vielbaum. *San Francisco's Municipal Railway: Muni*, Arcadia Publishing, Charleston, SC: 2011.

Wilson, Mark A. *Bernard Maybeck: Architect of Elegance*, Gibbs Smith, Layton, UT: 2011.

Wolf, Gary. *Wired: A Romance*, Random House, NY, NY: 2003.

Yung, Judy. *Unbound Voices: A Documentary History of Chinese Women in San Francisco*, University of California Press, Berkeley, CA: 1999.

von Zesch, Leonie. *Leonie: A Woman Ahead of Her Time*, Lime Orchard Publications, Studio City, CA: 2011.

IMAGE CREDITS

Museyon Guides would like to thank the following organizations and individuals for their guidance and assistance in creating *Chronicles of Old San Francisco*.

Boudin Bakery
California Historical Society
Cliff House Project
FoundSF
Library of Congress
National Park Service
The New Fillmore
Oakland Museum of California
San Francisco Heritage
San Francisco History Center, San Francisco Public Library
TCHO
UC Berkley, Bancroft Library
U.S. National Archives

Page 11:
Captain Juan Bautista Anza arrived at San Francisco Bay, Illustrations by David Rickman, courtesy of the National Park Service

Page 25:
View of San Francisco, formerly Yerba Buena, in 1846-7. Before the discovery of gold, c. 1884, Library of Congress, LC-DIG-pga-00251

Page 35:
Historic American Buildings Survey Wells Fargo Bank Historical Museum 1850 built 1850 - destroyed 1851 - Niantic Hotel, Historic View, Clay & Sansome Streets, San Francisco, San Francisco County, CA, Library of Congress, HABS CAL,38-SANFRA,40–1

Page 49:
Lotta Crabtree of the Old California Theater, 1876, San Francisco History Center, San Francisco Public Library

Page 61:
Mary Ellen ("Mammy") Pleasant at 87 years of age, San Francisco History Center, San Francisco Public Library

Page 70:
Chinese railroad workers and rocks, near opening of Summit Tunnel, between 1865 and 1869, Library of Congress, LC-DIG-stereo-1s00510

Page 75:
Cable Car on California Street, 1960s, San Francisco History Center, San Francisco Public Library

Page 76:
Andrew Hallidie suspension bridge, c. 1880, Library of Congress, HAER CAL,29-NEVCI,6–13

Page 83:
Ocean Beach after 1903, Courtesy of Cliff House Project

Page 87:
Golden Gate Park, Conservatory greenhouses in background, c. 1897, Library of Congress, LC-USZ62-70342

Page 89:
Music Pavillion, Golden Gate Park, c. 1902, Library of Congress, LC-USZ62-77078

Page 92:
A slave girl in holiday attire, Chinatown, San Francisco, 1896-1906, Arnold Genthe, Library of Congress, LC-G4033-0123

Page 105:
Cliff House, Little Miss Pierson on the beach, courtesy of Cliff House Project

Page 107:
Burning of the Call, The San Francisco Call newspaper building in flames after April 18, 1906 earthquake, Library of Congress, LC-USZ62-115694

Page 110:
Market Street toward ferry, 1906, Library of Congress, LC-DIG-det-4a13220

Page 111:
Home life among the refugees - a street of tents in the Presidio, 1906, Library of Congress, LC-DIG-ppmsca-09835

Page 113:
Fun making by the earthquake refugees—a group of people sitting outside of a decorated tent called the "House of Mirth" with signs indicating an available elevator and running water after the San Francisco earthquake in 1906, Library of Congress, LC-DIG-ppmsca-09837

Page 115:
Entrance to the Bank of America, 1943, Library of Congress, LC-USW3-024542-D

Page 116:
Ruins of the Bank of Italy building destroyed in the 1906 earthquake, April 19, 1906, San Francisco History Center, San Francisco Public Library

ABOUT MUSEYON

Named after the Museion, the ancient Egyptian institute dedicated to the muses, Museyon Guides is an independent publisher that explores the world through the lens of cultural obsessions. Intended for frequent fliers and armchair travelers alike, our books are expert-curated and carefully researched, offering rich visuals, practical tips and quality information.

MUSEYON'S OTHER TITLES

Pick one up and follow your interests...wherever they might go.
For more information vist **www.museyon.com**. www.facebook.com/museyon and www. twitter.com/museyon. Inquiries: info@museyon.com

MUSEYON INC.

Publisher: Akira Chiba
Editor: Heather Corcoran
Editor: Janice Battiste
Assistant Editor: Mackenzie Allison
Assistant Photo Editor: Misaki Matsui

Cover Design: José Antonio Contreras
Janis Joplin Cover Illustration: Eiko Imai
Design & Layout: CPI, Inc.
Assistant Designer: Shino Okawara
SN Marketing: Sara Marquez

Museyon Guides has made every effort to verify that all information included in this guide is accurate and current as of our press date. All details are subject to change.

ABOUT THE AUTHOR

Gael Chandler moved to San Francisco in 1970 to join the women's movement and liberate herself. After nine years in northern California, she left for Hollywood, where she edited dramas, documentaries and more and received two Cable ACE nominations for her cutting on a comedy series. In 2010, she returned to northern California where she continues her love affair with the City By The Bay and the land north of the Golden Gate Bridge—Marin and Sonoma counties.

Gael has written feature scripts and books: *Cut by Cut: Editing your Film or Video* and *Film Editing: Great Cuts Every Filmmaker and Movie Lover Must Know* and is always up for her next adventure—be it with words, places, or people. You can contact her and learn more about San Francisco then and now at her website, www.theSFstory.com.